The Doberman Pinscher

THE
DOBERMAN
PINSCHER

BY WOODROW KERFMANN

Title page: Glenayr Jamison, owned by Jay-Mee's Dobbies of Jamie and Ceci Martinez, and friend Christian.

Sections of this work have been adapted from *This is the Doberman Pinscher* by Louise Ziegler Spirer and Evelyn Miller and other pre-printed material from T.F.H. Publications.

Photo credits: Alexander, page 141; John L. Ashbey, pages 72, 76, 77, 100, 117, 128 (bottom), 150, 178; Richard Bergman, pages 173, 188; Martin Booth, page 224; William Brown, pages 23, 189, 190, 196; W. Bushman, pages 20, 167, 216 (bottom); Callea, page 59; C.M. Cooke & Son, pages 14 (bottom), 32, 34, 35, 36, 37, 50, 53; William P. Gilbert, pages 16, 154, 203; Norton Kent, pages 152, 216 (top); Carl Lindemaier, pages 85, 151, 193; Marsh, page 14 (top); Pan American World Airways, page 133; Don Petrulis, pages 120, 146; Vince Serbin, page 94; Evelyn M. Shafer, pages 8, 9, 18, 19, 21, 25, 161, 164, 171, 208, 221; Sally Anne Thompson, page 60; Three Lions, Inc., pages 118, 139, 228; Louise van der Meid. pages 44, 83, 90, 95, 99, 110, 123, 126, 152, 169, 183, 194, 204, 205, 214, 226, 241, 242, 244; Pierre Wilbaut, 29.

Distributed in the UNITED STATES by T.F.H. Publications, Inc., 211 West Sylvania Avenue, Neptune City, NJ 07753; in CANADA by H & L Pet Supplies Inc., 27 Kingston Crescent, Kitchener, Ontario N2B 2T6; Rolf C. Hagen Ltd., 3225 Sartelon Street, Montreal 382 Quebec; in ENGLAND by T.F.H. Publications Limited, 4 Kier Park, Ascot, Berkshire SL5 7DS; in AUSTRALIA AND THE SOUTH PACIFIC by T.F.H. (Australia) Pty. Ltd., Box 149, Brookvale 2100 N.S.W., Australia; in NEW ZEALAND by Ross Haines & Son, Ltd., 18 Monmouth Street, Grey Lynn, Auckland 2 New Zealand; in SINGAPORE AND MALAYSIA by MPH Distributors (S) Pte., Ltd., 601 Sims Drive, # 03/07/21, Singapore 1438; in the PHILIPPINES by Bio-Research, 5 Lippay Street, San Lorenzo Village, Makati Rizal; in SOUTH AFRICA by Multipet Pty. Ltd., 30 Turners Avenue, Durban 4001. Published by T.F.H. Publications Inc. Manufactured in the United States of America by T.F.H. Publications, Inc.

The Dobermann Pinscher Klub of Germany was founded in 1912, by which time interest in showing Dobermanns (as the breed is now known in Germany) had reached the point where 105 of them had competed at the 1910 big dog show in Cologne.

Germany has played a vital role in the development of Doberman Pinschers throughout the world. Importations from there have been involved in the breeding programs wherever the breed is known, and they have been used to develop true quality. The modern Doberman is no longer a ferocious animal as in the early days of its development. Selective breeding has created an ideal, as well as beautiful, companion who is intelligent and steady as a guard dog, handsome, well balanced, strong, and elegant to the eye.

In Other Countries

Switzerland's first Doberman Pinscher Club was founded in 1902. The Swiss are said to have appreciated the breed's adaptability to all weather conditions and the fact that its short coat dries quickly and is odor-free. We understand that in the beginning the Swiss people feared the breed due to some overly aggressive dogs who at first came there; but careful training and selective breeding soon corrected the situation, the Doberman then quickly gaining a position of admiration and respect. The "mother of Dobermans" in Switzerland was a very famous bitch, Miss Bernacki, who produced numerous puppies in her more than several litters.

Holland quickly followed in adoption of the breed, and by 1909 Dobermans had migrated there, where they achieved instant popularity. Another early area to welcome the Doberman was the Dutch East Indies, where, despite the climate, they flourished. We understand that there is still at least one Specialty club active there today.

It did not take long for appreciation of the Doberman to arise throughout all of Europe. Austria, Belgium, France, and Italy all had early Specialty clubs involved in the promotion of these dogs. Strangely, acceptance in England was more slowly reached, probably due to the dropped ears since cropping is forbidden in that country. In the United States and Canada, Dobermans have long been acknowledged with admiration and their rise in popularity has been steady. Also there is tremendous activity in Australia, despite the ear-cropping ban similar to England's.

Grand Champion Danica Stamm's Juon winning Best in Show at the Eurodog-show with the judge, Avik Marshak of Israel. Owned by Mr. and Mrs. Mulero, Dompierre/Mer, France.

This is the famous Doberman who went to Japan where he became Grand Champion Mikadobe's Mikado v d Elbe. Photo, taken in 1952 by Aoki, loaned to us by Mrs. Mae L. Downing, Mikadobe Kennels, Marietta, Georgia.

In Modern Times

The Doberman was intended as a working dog—to be used for guard work, sentry duty, shepherding and as a watch dog. We doubt if people at home use their Dobermans to herd sheep, but they certainly can be fine watch dogs and protectors of hearth and home.

Many Dobermans, however, are trained by the police and military as guard dogs and war dogs.

Perhaps the Doberman is best known for his work with the armed forces. With his intelligence, alertness, and physical prowess, he can be easily trained for such work.

We have evidence that the ancient Assyrians, Persians, Greeks, and Romans used war dogs. By 1910 the British were training dogs for both sentry and rescue work. The Germans, using both Dobermans and German Shepherds, had 6,000 dogs in service by 1914.

13

Ch. Dictator von Glenhugel, bred by John Cholley, and owned by Peggy and Bob Adamson.

English Ch. Challenger of Sonhende, owned by R.H. Jackson.

A lovely Doberman from Australia, Ch. Tanunda Sportsaction, owned by Mrs. M. Hart, Kellyville, New South Wales. Pictured at the Doberman Specialty Show in 1980.

The Doberman performed many heroic tasks during his war service, but perhaps his most important activity was rescuing the wounded. There is evidence that at least 4,000 soldiers were first found by trained dogs. The dogs were taught that if they found a man in a prone position, they were to go back to their master and lead him to the wounded man.

Dogs were even used to find enemy positions. The U.S. Marine Corps has reason to be proud of its K-9 dog corps, the "Devil Dogs." Six dogs, four of them Dobermans, were cited for their work in the South Pacific. These dogs "hit the beach" with the Marines.

"Andy" saved a Marine tank platoon by locating the Japanese gun nests which were harassing the group. "Otto" and "Rex" warned their masters of Japanese snipers and located their gun positions. Many servicemen were saved by these fearless dogs!

But the Doberman is equally at home in less war-like places. Some are used as Seeing Eye dogs, others as night watchmen, but most are family dogs. Unfortunately, because of his war work, the Doberman is sometimes feared. As every Doberman owner knows, this is far from the truth. Your Doberman has more than his share of the qualities of "man's best friend." Affectionate, fond of children, playful, and loyal, and with great intelligence, he is a perfect member of the household.

15

Ch. Elfred's Golden Nugget owned by Kandy Berley, handled by Robert S. Forsyth.

Chapter 2

Doberman Pinschers in the United States

The first Doberman Pinscher to be registered in the United States was named Doberman Intelectus, the only one of the breed registered in that year, 1908. He was a black and tan dog born that same year, owned by Carl Schulyheiss, sired by a German import, Bertel v. Hohenstein (whose name had been changed to Doberman Bertel), from a German bitch (also Hohenstein) known in America as Doberman Hertha.

The bitch, Doberman Hertha, in 1912 went down on the records as the first of her breed to become an American Kennel Club champion. The first Doberman *dog* to complete title in the United States was an American-bred male, Champion Doberman Dix.

It is interesting to make special note about the kennel prefix of these dogs. "Doberman" had been granted as a kennel prefix in 1908 to Theodore F. Jager from Pittsford, New York, something which could not happen now as the American Kennel Club has long since discontinued the use of a breed name as a kennel prefix. The Doberman Kennel, as noted from the number of firsts it attained, was a busy organization in its day and must have made a number of people aware of the breed.

By the beginning of World War I, numerous people were breeding Dobermans in various parts of the United States, and an early Doberman Pinscher Club of America was organized during this period.

It was after the close of World War I, and getting into the 1920's, that Dobermans truly started to hit their stride in the United States.

The magnificent winning Doberman of the late 1950s and early 1960s, Ch. Ebonaire's Touchdown, owned by Charles A.T. O'Neill and handled by J. Monroe Stebbins. This dog was a noted and consistent winner at prestigious shows in keenest competition.

The present Doberman Pinscher Club of America came into being following a meeting in New York in February 1921; it has grown to well over a thousand members by now and is one of the most truly prestigious, concerned, helpful, and active breed Specialty clubs to be found anywhere. Their program is an inspiration and could well serve as an example to be followed by those in many other breeds.

But returning to the dogs themselves!

During the 1920's, no matter what the breed in which one was interested, importations were brought over in droves from Great Britain and Europe, to be used in the establishment of energetic young American kennels. To this end, Dobermans were no exception, and throughout that decade, well into the 1930's, Siegers and Siegerins came here to the extent that it almost seemed as though none possibly could be left in Germany. It is to the credit of our American breeders that they

This lovely bitch is Ch. Tait's Miss Scoreboard handled by J. Monroe Stebbins to Winners Bitch at the Quaker City Doberman Pinscher Club Specialty Show in December 1962.

used these imports well, bred from them intelligently, and in due course brought the American-bred Doberman to the point where it could compete successfully with members of the breed from any part of the world.

The first of the notable imports was brought over by George F. Earle of Pennsylvania in 1921 for his Red Roof Kennels. He was Champion Lord v.d. Hortsburg, whom we have heard described as an excellent dog used frequently at stud.

The first Sieger to come to America was Benno v. Burgholz in 1923.

It was during the early 1920's that a gentleman who was to become one of the breed's foremost authorities, Mr. Francis F.H. Fleitmann, imported from Holland Champion Prinz Karlo v.d. Konigstad. It was a grandson of this dog, Champion Carlo of Rhinegold, who became the first American-bred Doberman to win Best in Show.

WESTCHESTER KENNEL CLUB
D.P.C. CONN. N.Y. SPECIALTY
SEPTEMBER 11, 1966
JUDGE MISS ANNA K. NICHOLAS
BEST
OF
BREED
* A BUSHMAN PHOTO *

A memorable Best in Show Doberman bitch, Ch. Tarra's Aventina, winning one of her Specialty Show Bests of Breed for Mr. and Mrs. Frank D'Amico, handled by Jane Kamp Forsyth.

The great Ch. Rancho Dobe's Storm in 1952 with his handler, A. Peter Knoop. This fantastic dog was owned by Mr. and Mrs. Len Carey and was highly influential in the present day breeding programs in both England and Australia and a dog of importance here in the United States. Storm was one of only six dogs of any breed ever to have twice won Best in Show at the prestigious Westminster Kennel Club event.

Mr. Fleitmann's Westphalia Kennels became one of the most important in the breed, producing magnificent dogs on a steady basis and providing foundation stock for many other breeders.

Another important breeder, Glenn S. Stains, imported Lux v.d. Blankenburg for his Pontchartrain Kennels during the mid-1920's, this despite the fact that the dog at the time of purchase was already eight years old. The dominance of this dog was tremendous! Both in the United States and in Germany the producing powers of his progeny were fantastic, and he very definitely takes his place in Doberman history as one of the most influential and important of all sires.

Champion Troll v.d. Engelsburg was another memorable Doberman to come to the United States. In Germany he sired Siegers Ferry and Freya v. Rauhfelsen and was imported by E. Bornstein. Troll's

Alisaton Maserati, by Ch. Glenyr Dufferinand ex Ch. Alisaton Kindewicke is one of the many fine Dobermans handled by Terry Lazzaro, Gaylordsville, Ct.

The sensational winning bitch of the late 1960s-early 1970s. Ch. Aventina's Tamiko owned by Frank and Ellie D'Amico winning the Working Group under the late Alva Rosenberg at Newton Kennel Club, August 1970, Jane Forsyth handling.

25

Canadian Ch. Roger V. Franconia, C.D. Owned by Mrs. Ellen Hoffmann.

Chapter 3

Doberman Pinschers in Canada

Doberman Pinschers were popular in Canada back in the 1940's, since which time they have continued to flourish there. Even earlier than that, during the late 1930's, Dr. Wilfred Shute had formed his Mannerheim Kennels, mainly on stock imported from the United States, and he was to become a memorable breeder who made a valuable contribution to Dobes. Included in his foundation stock was American and Canadian Champion Defender of Jan-Har who sired more than twenty champions along with accumulating notable show records.

Dr. Shute bred many Dobes who achieved fame and exemplified quality, among them were Champion Adam (a Group winner), Champion Dixie (Best in Show winner and a top producing bitch), and American and Canadian Champion Renco.

Another breeder from the 1930's, this one in Nova Scotia, started Trollhattan Kennels. This gentleman is Harvey Gratton. Champion Tarrado's Chaos has been an important producer for this kennel. He was purchased from the United States during the late 1960's and he, too, produced more than twenty champions for his owner.

At the present time there are numerous Canadian kennels featuring Dobermans most successfully from coast to coast.

The popular Canadian professional handler Harold Butler, from Quebec, has piloted many a famous Canadian Doberman to victory. He, too, is a long-time Dobe fancier, having co-owned some with Dr. Shute and also having handled for Kaukauna Kennels owned by Mrs. Kay England.

Present-day Canadian breeders include the Simca Kennels at Nobleton, Ontario, which was founded on Canadian and American Cham-

Canadian Ch. Simca's April Wine, owner-handled by Lana Sniderman, Simca Kennels, to a Group placement.

Judgar's High Esteem, handsome young Doberman winning Best Puppy in Show at the Thousand Islands Kennel Club in 1980. By Ch. Jagermeister High Noon ex Judgar's Lady Amazon, High Esteem was bred by G. and J. Kauffeldt, owned by Wayne Hedges of Orleans, Ontario, Canada, and handled by Donna Fraser.

pion Sherluck's Crimson 'n' Clover and which is meeting with very satisfactory success. Crimson 'n' Clover is herself an all-breed Best in Show winner and her progeny have included Canadian Champion Simca's April Wine, Doberman Pinscher Club of America Grand Prize Futurity Winner; Canadian Champion Simca's Almost Like Flying; Canadian Champion Simca's Asleep At The Wheel; Canadian and American Champion Simca's Amanda Trees; and others who are on their way to fame. Lana Sniderman and Bob Krol own the Simca Dobes and are enthusiastically making plans for the future of their splendid dogs.

Jaegermeister Kennels, at Spencerville, Ontario, were founded in the forties by Fred J. Heal, and the bloodlines there have been developed on the Schauffelein strain through Canadian and Bermuda Champion Schauffelein's Shady Lady, C.D.X., who was to become Canada's top winning female of all time. She was bred back to her sire,

This Best in Show and multiple Group placing Canadian Doberman is Champion Dobermien's Virgo, proudly owned and enjoyed by the Michel Plamondons, Lac Beauport, Quebec. Here winning a Working Group in 1983 handled by noted professional Harold Butler.

Canadian and American Champion Schauffelein's Troll Arabasque, and produced one of the finest producing bitches from this kennel, Champion Jagermeister's Renown. This mother and daughter have truly left their mark on the breed through some very outstanding and famous progeny.

Solar Kennels, Woodstock, Ontario, are owned by Allan and Jane Marshall who started raising Dobermans in 1971 after eighteen years of raising Boxers. Their bitch, Champion Solar's Toronado, was selected as one of the Top Twenty Dogs in Canada for the year August 1977 to July 31st 1978, a very exciting honor! This was followed by her being Top Doberman Bitch in all of Canada for the next four years. Then in 1980 this same bitch was chosen Dog of the Year by the Doberman Pinscher Club of Canada, and in 1983 she won four Bests in Show along with numerous Group placements bringing her points to a level which will very likely lead to her again being Top Doberman Pinscher in 1983.

Douglas Ringstrom, Star Storm Dobermans in Calgary, owns American and Canadian Champion Starstorm Thunderbolt, American and Canadian C.D. This dog was the Top Stud among Dobermans in Canada for the years 1980 through 1983, with over 60 Canadian champion offspring, five American champions, and a South African champion to his credit at the time of his death at the very early age of six years. A multiple Best in Show and Specialty winner in Canada, he held an Award of Merit from the Doberman Pinscher Club of America and had some splendid wins to his credit in the United States. He also was the winner of High in Trial at the 1982 Doberman Pinscher Club of America Specialty.

A.E. (Bud) and Wendy Beck own Dawnaquinn Kennels at Calgary, founded on Kay Hill and Satan lines. The Becks have two Dobes which they personally owner-handled to Best in Show victories, and they have produced more than 30 champions despite a limited breeding program. Champion Free Spirits Quinnella, C.D., was their foundation bitch. American and Canadian Champion Dawnaquinn's John Galt and Champion Dawnaquinn's Day Dream Rose are the two with whom they so far have won Best in Show.

These are just a few of the people and dogs making Canadian Doberman history. You will find more details and kennel stories on Dobermans everywhere in the new forthcoming T.F.H. book *The World of the Doberman Pinscher* written by Anna Katherine Nicholas and scheduled for release during 1985.

English Ch.
Bowesmoor
Mona, owned by
G.D. Thompson.

English Ch.
Jupiter of Tavey,
owned by A.B.
Hogg.

32

Chapter 4

Doberman Pinschers in Great Britain

Dobermans did not attract any great attention in English dog show circles until about 1950, prior to which time they were relegated to the "Any other breed not separately classified" status at the shows. Following the close of World War II their primary function in Great Britain was as a working dog, used by the police and by the armed forces for guard duty. Slowly all that changed, however, with German Shepherds gaining greater demand for those activities (although the Dobermans were highly satisfactory, intelligent, and useful workers); and the dog show world became increasingly aware of the Doberman's attributes.

The earliest English Doberman breeding stock came, of course, from Germany. Some Dobes also came from Holland and Switzerland. Then the British started to appreciate the strides American breeders had been making and started to import some leading American bloodlines, using them well to improve show type and elegance.

Three Dobermans went to England from the United States during 1952. These were Damasyn Sirocco, by the famous American Champion Dictator v. Glenhugal ex Damasyn The Song, bred by Peggy Adamson and Mrs. R.C. Polak; Lady Gretchen, by West Hill Adonis ex Gretchen, bred by Mrs. F.W. Streck; and Quita of Jerry Run, a blue bitch bred by Mrs. Rhys Carpenter from Arbleau of Jerry Run ex Oenone of Jerry Run.

Four years later, in 1956, Mrs. J. Curnow imported the first American champion Doberman into England. He was Champion Rustic Adagio, by American Champion Kilburn Ideal (Marge Kilburn is one

English Ch. Tavey's Stormy Nugget, owned by F. Williams.

of America's most notable and successful breeders of Dobermans) ex Rustic Kiser; and although of Kilburn stock, this dog was bred by G.F. Kiser. Mrs. Curnow has probably brought more Dobes from the United States to England than any other single British Dobe breeder (probably due to the fact that she and her husband frequently have visited the United States over the years on judging assignments and thus were personally familiar with and aware of what American breeders were producing).

Later in the 1950's, Mrs. Curnow brought over Orebaugh's Raven of Taber, a daughter of Champion Rancho Dobe's Primo (thus a half-sister to American Champion Rancho Dobe's Storm) ex Champion Orebaugh's Gentian. Then around the mid-sixties Vanessa's Little Dictator (Champion Checkmate's Chessman ex Champion Valheim's Vanessa) and Westwinds Quintessence (Elblac Zaturno ex Westwinds

English Ch. Tavey's Stormy Objection, owned by M. Ferraro-Cini.

Majoram) were added to her kennel. Still later imports by Mrs. Curnow included Distinctive Daneen (American Champion Marks-Tey's Hanover ex American Champion Dodie of Marks-Tey, C.D.) in co-ownership with E. Hoxey, Arawak Perfecta (American Champion Dolph Von Tannenwald ex Arawak Hi-A-Leah, C.D.), and Camiereich Day Trip To Tavey (American Champion Kay Hill's Takeswon to Knowon ex American Champion Study Halls Smarti of Kay Hill), the latter two in the 1970's.

Among other British importations from the United States were Highbriar Olympik (American Champion Florian Von Ahrtal, C.D.X., ex American Champion Highbriar Blackbird, C.D.X.) to A. Billingham; GraLemor Freebooter (American Champion Marks-Tey Shawn, C.D., ex GraLemor Eve of Destiny) to Robert H. Walker; Champion Beau James of Rustic Gold (Aladean of Philcra Lane ex

American Champion Rustic Gold); Taylor's Flamme Warlock (American Champion Underhill's Roc Von Warlock, C.D., ex Lowell's Contessa Rhea), imported in whelp to American Champion Aztec's Beacon and owned by Connie Jo Taylor; Amsel's Andante of Marks-Tey (American Champion Marks-Tey Shawn, C.D., ex American Champion Hanover's Amsel, C.D.) to Robert H. Walker; and Kay Hill's Outrigger (American Champion Dolph von Tannenwald ex Kay Hill's Kay a Maran) to Mrs. E. Edwards.

Presently breeding Dobermans in England are Tavey Kennels, now owned by Reg and Mary Barton, whose kennels trace their beginnings back to the 1950's; Bellmarsh Dobermans, owned by Mrs. B.A. Rowland; Antara Dobermans, owned by John and Rita Carlisle; Milperra Dobermans, owned by Mrs. Vicki Cuthbertson; and numerous others.

English Ch. Carickgreen Walda Negasta, owned by D.P. Clark.

English Ch.
Tumslow Storm
Caesar, owned by
G.F. Platt.

English Ch.
Precept of Tavey,
owned by Mrs.
W.M. Cathcart.

Australian Ch. Windswept Blue Bootees, a Best in Show winner owned by Windswept Dobermans, Sheridan Pausey, Blackton, New South Wales, Australia.

Chapter 5

Doberman Pinschers in Australia

Australian fanciers are great dog lovers, and many breeds are owned and being bred there with marked success. Among them is the Doberman Pinscher, where the foundation stock came from England with later crosses from America and Europe. Doberman interest in Australia would seem to date from sometime during the 1950's, and by 1959 Doberman breeders had produced some serious contenders at Australian dog shows. The imports from the United States have been given credit for their influence on the modern Australian Doberman and for the excellence of the many handsome and high quality champions Australian Dobe breeders are now producing.

The earliest Dobermans imported into Australia for show purposes were owned by Mr. Pilko of Sydney in New South Wales. Dobermans were entered for the first time at the Sydney Royal Easter Show during 1952, with the Melbourne Royal's first Doberman entries coming in 1954. In 1959 a Doberman bitch, Champion Carmenita Dianna, won the Best Exhibit in Group award at the Melbourne Royal.

Among the early stock imported from Great Britain, special note must be made of Champion Tavey's Stormy Accolade, who came from one of England's finest kennels, Tavey, owned by those widely esteemed authorities Mr. and Mrs. Fred Curnow. Accolade was one of a litter sired by the immortal American Champion Rancho Dobe's Storm and born in quarantine. Although imported from an English kennel he represented the highest quality American bloodlines, I believe the first of these to be used in Australia.

A very influential dog in the development of Australian-bred Dobermans was Ebonaire's Bravo, who came from the famed Ebonaire Ken-

Australian Ch. Windswept Baby Doll as a ten-month-old puppy. Sheridan Pausey, owner.

nels owned by Edward and Judy Weiss on Long Island, New York, where so many highly influential Dobes have been produced. His Australian owners were Mr. and Mrs. T. Farmilo and M. McNicholl, and he certainly justified their selection of him! Bravo sired 45 champions, among them the notable Australian-bred Champion Koning Brave Lustre who achieved the most striking of all early Doberman victories in Australia when she was awarded Best in Show, all-breeds, at the Melbourne Royal, the highest award at a Royal Show to be accorded the breed until then.

The earliest Doberman activity in Australia was evidently based in Melbourne, but we note a steady spreading out to all parts of the country.

Ebonaire's Bravo was a son of the famed Champion Steb's Top Skipper from Ebonaire's On Guard.

Windswept Baby Bunting at ten years. The sire of five champions, owned, bred and loved by Sheridan Pausey, Windswept Dobermans, Australia.

In Australia, Dobermans compete in the Non-Sporting Group, which consists of most breeds shown in the Working Group in the United States, plus Boxers, Danes, Poodles, Miniature Schnauzers, and so on, making it the largest and probably most competitive of all Australian variety groups.

We have in our possession the catalogue of the Royal Agricultural Society Kennel Control 1983 Spring Fair Dog Show, which reveals some interesting facts about Dobermans in Australia today. The Doberman entry consisted of close to 90 individual dogs. Best of Breed and the bitch Challenge Certificate were awarded to Australian Champion Stehle Binda, born in May 1981, a daughter of Australian Champion Stehle King, C.D., ex Australian Champion Summersky Eliza. The Challenge Certificate for dogs was won by Australian Champion

Shato Norwegian Wood, born October 1976, by Australian Champion Tanunda Royal Bacchus ex Vreedenburg Czarina. Stehle Binda belongs to D. and Mrs. A. Eschbach. Shato Norwegian Wood is owned by Mrs. L. Kann.

Reserve Challenge in bitches at this event was awarded to Australian Champion Katenburg Mikaela, born August 1978, by Lynmara Lucifer ex Katenburg Miss Jessy, owned by A.R. and Mrs. J. Mercer; in dogs, the Reserve Challenge went to Meliora Brazil, born June 1980, by Australian Champion Bikila Fire Ablaze ex Meliora Casino, owned by R. and Mrs. L. McDonald.

Among the other Dobermans of note entered at this show were, in dogs, Champion Erandobe Zanuck, by Deerfields Salute to Kay Hill (imported from Canada) ex Erandobe My Fair Lady, born June 1981, owned by E. and Mrs. A.M. Appleby; Champion Bowerbank Eagle, by Australian Champion Bikila Genghis Khan ex Bikila Funny Girl, born April 1981, owned by Mrs. S. Trist; Champion Meliora Brazil Carajas, by Australian Champion Bikila Fire Ablaze ex Meliora Casino, born June 1980, owned by K.O. Adamson; Champion Firezan Attila The Hun, by Australian Champion Bikila Genghis Khan ex Australian Champion Bikila Femme Fatale, born July 1979, owned by D.P. and Mrs. A.D. Bowe; Champion Lebensmut Saraband, by Australian Champion Tanunda Laras Wrath ex Lebansmut Sues Replica, born August 1978, owned by P. and Mrs. P. Fraser; Champion Tanunda Sportsaction, by Australian Champion Shato Norwegian Wood (Challenge Certificate winner at this show) ex Australian Champion Tanunda Anastasia, born July 1979, owned by Mrs. M.B. Hart; Champion Shato Mullingar, C.D., by Australian Champion Tanunda Laras Wrath ex Australian Champion Tanunda Autumn Wonder, born October 1979, owned by Miss J.M. Jones; Champion Maharighi Panache, by Borealis Midday Sun ex Australian Champion Maharighi Aminah, born June 1980, owned by F.S.L. and Mrs. M. Price; Champion Artemus Bee Jay, by Australian Champion Tanunda Laras Wrath ex Tanunda High Fashion, born June 1980, owned by S. Smith; Champion Vondobe Destroyer, by Deerfields Salute to Kay Hill (Canadian import) ex Australian Champion Tavey's Elsinore (United Kingdom import), born September 1979, owned by N.D. and Mrs. N.J. Wenban; and Champion Borealis El Khedive, by Australian Champion Rama the Ramadan ex Australian Champion Borealis Neat Bianca, born March 1977, owned by L.C. and Mrs. M. Wheeler.

In bitches the entries at this Royal included, in addition to those already mentioned, Champion Bowerbank Elegance, by Australian Champion Bikila Genghis Khan ex Bikila Funny Girl, born April 1981, owned by D.P. and Mrs. A.D. Bowe (littermate to Champion Bowerbank Eagle); Champion Meliora Crown Opal, by Australian Champion Bikila Fire Ablaze ex Meliora Casino, born September 1981, owned by Mrs. C.G. Egan; Champion Prussian Divorcee, by Champion Shato Norwegian Wood (dog Challenge Certificate winner at this show) ex Prussian Sabre Charm, born December 1980, owned by A.K. and Mrs. C.J. Parziani; Champion Adelwin Drusilla, by Lynmara Lucifer ex Australian Champion Steigerwald Carla, born January 1980, owned by V.G. and Mrs. R.J. Burns; Champion Dobeherr Star Dazzla, by Australian Champion Starrae Black Legend ex Australian Champion Dobeherr Fire Dancer, born October 1981, owned by Dobeherr Kennels; Champion Tanunda Thorgerda, by Australian Champion Shato Norwegian Wood (winner of Dog Challenge Certificate at this show) ex Tanunda Funny Girl, born November 1981, owned by Mrs. M.B. Hart; Champion Meliora Crown Jewel, by Champion Bikila Fire Ablaze ex Meliora Casino, born September 1981, owned by Meliora Kennels; Champion Sonza Black Magic, C.D., by Australian Champion Silvanglen Super Star ex Zedekiah Lady Leah, C.D., born October 1980, owned by Mrs. S.C. Montgomery; Champion Silvanglen Centrefold, by Australian, English and Irish Champion Kenstaff Tornado of Achenburg (United Kingdom import) ex Australian Champion Udelewar Mariah, born July 1980, owned by M. and Mrs. L. Parrish; Champion Prussian Red Hot Miss, by Tanunda Baccarat ex Steigerwald Felicity, born September 1979, owned by A.K. and Mrs. C.J. Parziani; and Champion Borealis Bathsheba, C.D., by Australian Champion Rama The Ramadan ex Australian Champion Borealis Neat Bianca, born March 1977, owned by L.C. and Mrs. M. Wheeler.

A good male Doberman head seen directly from the front.

Chapter 6

Standards of the Doberman Pinscher

A breed standard is basically a description of an ideal specimen of the breed. No dog can be the complete ideal, but show winners are generally those dogs which come closest to the ideal. If you are buying a dog for show purposes, it is wise to check the points you need. Even if you just want a dog for the home, you may still want to purchase a dog which conforms closely to the standard, for some day you may wish your dog to have a litter. Selecting your dog carefully also discourages those unscrupulous breeders who are turning out dogs with little regard for the quality of the breed.

A *fault* is a departure from the ideal. It is not enough to disqualify a dog from the show ring, but it hurts his chances of winning.

A *disqualifying fault* disqualifies a dog from showing. It is of a more serious nature than a fault.

American Standard

The American Kennel Club sets the standards for all breeds of pedigreed dogs in the United States. The standard by which the Doberman is judged was drawn up by the Doberman Pinscher Club of America and approved by the Board of Directors of the American Kennel Club.

GENERAL CONFORMATION AND APPEARANCE: The appearance is that of a dog of medium size, with a body that is square; the height, measured virtually from the ground to the highest point of the withers, equalling the length measured horizontally from the fore-chest to the rear projection of the upper thigh.

HEIGHT at the withers: *Dogs*—26 to 28 inches, ideal about 27½ inches; *Bitches*—24 to 26 inches, ideal about 25½ inches. Length of head, neck and legs in proportion to length and depth of body. Compactly built, muscular and powerful, for great endurance and speed. Elegant in appearance, of proud carriage, reflecting great nobility and temperament. Energetic, watchful, determined, alert, fearless, loyal and obedient.

The judge shall dismiss from the ring any shy or vicious Doberman.

SHYNESS: A dog shall be judged fundamentally shy if, refusing to stand for examination, it shrinks away from the judge; if it fears an approach from the rear; if it shies at sudden and unusual noises to a marked degree.

VICIOUSNESS: A dog that attacks or attempts to attack either the judge or its handler, is definitely vicious. An aggressive or belligerent attitude towards other dogs shall not be deemed viciousness.

HEAD: Long and dry, resembling a blunt wedge in both frontal and profile views. When seen from the front, the head widens gradually toward the base of the ears in a practically unbroken line. Top of skull flat, turning with slight stop to bridge of muzzle, with muzzle line extending parallel to top line of skull. Cheeks flat and muscular. Lips lying close to jaws. Jaws full and powerful, well filled under the eyes.

EYES: Almond shaped, moderately deep set, with vigorous, energetic expression. Iris, of uniform color, ranging from medium to darkest brown in black dogs; in reds, blues, and fawns the color of the iris blends with that of the markings, the darkest shade being preferable in every case.

TEETH: Strongly developed and white. Lower incisors upright and touching inside of upper incisors—a true scissors bite. *42 correctly placed teeth,* 22 in the lower, 20 in the upper jaw. Distemper teeth shall not be penalized. *Disqualifying Faults*—Overshot more than 3/16 of an inch. Undershot more than 1/8 of an inch. Four or more missing teeth.

EARS: Normally cropped and carried erect. The upper attachment of the ear, when held erect, is on a level with the top of the skull.

NECK: Proudly carried, well muscled and dry. Well arched, with nape of neck widening gradually toward body. Length of neck proportioned to body and head.

BODY: Back short, firm, of sufficient width, and muscular at the loins, extending in a straight line from withers to the *slightly* rounded croup. *Withers*—pronounced and forming the highest point of the body. *Brisket*—reaching deep to the elbow. *Chest*—broad with fore-chest well defined. *Ribs*—well sprung from the spine, but flattened in lower end to permit elbow clearance. *Belly*—well tucked up, extending in a curved line from the brisket. *Loins*—wide and muscled. *Hips*—broad and in proportion to body, breadth of hips being approximately equal to breadth of body at rib cage and shoulders.

TAIL: Docked at approximately second joint, appears to be a continuation of the spine, and is carried only slightly above the horizontal when the dog is alert.

FOREQUARTERS: *Shoulder Blade*—sloping forward and downward at a 45-degree angle to the ground meets the upper arm at an angle of 90 degrees. Length of shoulder blade and upper arm are equal. Height from elbow to withers approximately equals height from ground to elbow. *Legs*—seen from front and side, perfectly straight and parallel to each other from elbow to pastern; muscled and sinewy, with heavy bone. In normal pose and when gaiting, the elbows lie close to the brisket. *Pasterns*—firm and almost perpendicular to the ground. *Feet*—well arched, compact, and catlike, turning neither in nor out. Dewclaws may be removed.

HINDQUARTERS: The angulation of the hindquarters balances that of the forequarters. *Hip Bone*—falls away from spinal column at an angle of about 30 degrees, producing a slightly rounded, well-filled-out croup. *Upper Shanks*—at right angles to the hip bones, are long, wide, and well muscled on both sides of thigh, with clearly defined stifles. Upper and lower shanks are of equal length. While the dog is at rest, hock to heel is perpendicular to the ground. Viewed from the rear, the legs are straight, parallel to each other, and wide enough apart to fit in with a properly built body. *Cat Feet*—as on front legs, turning neither in nor out. Dewclaws, if any, are generally removed.

GAIT: Free, balanced, and vigorous, with good reach in the forequarters and good driving power in the hindquarters. When trotting, there is strong rear-action drive. Each rear leg moves in line with the foreleg on the same side. Rear and front legs are thrown neither in nor out. Back remains strong and firm. When moving at a fast trot, a properly built dog will single-track.

COAT, COLOR, MARKINGS: *Coat*—smooth-haired, short, hard, thick and close lying. Invisible gray undercoat on neck permissible. *Allowed Colors*—Black, red, blue, and fawn (Isabella). *Markings*—Rust, sharply defined, appearing above each eye and on muzzle, throat and

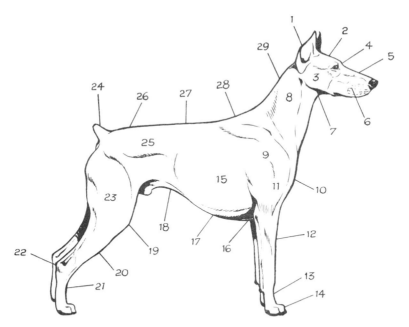

External Anatomy of the Doberman Pinscher: 1. Ears; 2. Forehead (skull); 3. Cheek; 4. Stop; 5. Foreface; 6. Muzzle; 7. Throat; 8. Neck; 9. Shoulder; 10. Fore Chest; 11. Upper Arm (part of shoulder assembly); 12. Fore Leg; 13. Pastern; 14. Front Foot; 15. Chest Cavity and Ribbing; 16. Elbow; 17. Brisket; 18. Belly; 19. Stifle (knee joint); 20. Lower Thigh; 21. Hock; 22. Hock Joint; 23. Thigh; 24. Tail (stern); 25. Loin; 26. Croup; 27. Back; 28. Withers; 29. Crest (of neck). Drawing by Ernest Hart.

forechest, on all legs and feet, and below tail. *Nose*—Solid black on black dogs, dark brown on red ones, dark gray on blue ones, dark tan on fawns. White patch on chest, not exceeding ½ square inch, permissible. *Disqualifying Fault*—Dogs not of an allowed color.

FAULTS
The foregoing description is that of the ideal Doberman Pinscher. Any deviation from the above described dog must be penalized to the extent of the deviation.

DISQUALIFICATIONS
Overshot more than 3/16 of an inch; undershot more than 1/8 of an inch. Four or more missing teeth. Dogs not of an allowed color.

British Standard

The Kennel Club sets the standards for all breeds of pedigreed dogs in Great Britain. This dog breed is known simply as the Dobermann in Great Britain.

CHARACTERISTICS: The Dobermann is a dog of good medium size with a well-set body, muscular and elegant. He has a proud carriage and a bold, alert temperament. His form is compact and tough and owing to his build capable of great speed. His gait is light and elastic. His eyes show intelligence and firmness of character, and he is loyal and obedient. Shyness or viciousness must be heavily penalised.

HEAD AND SKULL: Has to be proportionate to the body. It must be long, well filled under the eyes and clean cut. Its form seen from above and from the side must resemble a blunt wedge. The upper part of the head should be as flat as possible and free from wrinkle. The top of the skull should be flat with a slight stop, and the muzzle line extend parallel to the top line of the skull. The cheeks must be flat and the lips tight. The nose should be solid black in black dogs, solid dark brown in brown dogs, and solid dark grey in blue dogs. Head out of balance in proportion to body, dish-faced, snipy or cheeky should be penalised.

EYES: Should be almond-shaped, not round, moderately deep set, not prominent, with vigorous, energetic expression. Iris of uniform colour, ranging from medium to darkest brown in black dogs, the darker shade being the more desirable. In browns or blues the colour of the iris should blend with that of the markings, but not be of lighter hue than that of the markings. Light eyes in black dogs to be discouraged.

EARS: Should be small, neat and set high on the head. Erect or dropped, but erect preferred.

MOUTH: Should be very well developed, solid and strong, with a scissor bite. The incisors of the lower jaw must touch the inner face of the incisors of the upper jaw. Overshot or undershot mouths, badly arranged or decayed teeth to be penalised.

NECK: Should be fairly long and lean, carried erect and with considerable nobility, slightly convex and proportionate to the whole shape of the dog. The region of the nape has to be muscular. Dewlap and loose skin are undesirable.

FOREQUARTERS: The shoulder blade and upper arm should meet at an angle of 90 degrees. Relative length of shoulder and upper arm should be as one, excess length of upper arm being much less undesirable than excess length of shoulder blade. The legs, seen from

49

English Ch.
Tumlow Fantasy,
owned by Miss E.
Hoxey.

English Ch.
Tavey's Stormy
Abundance,
owned by Mrs. J.
Curnow.

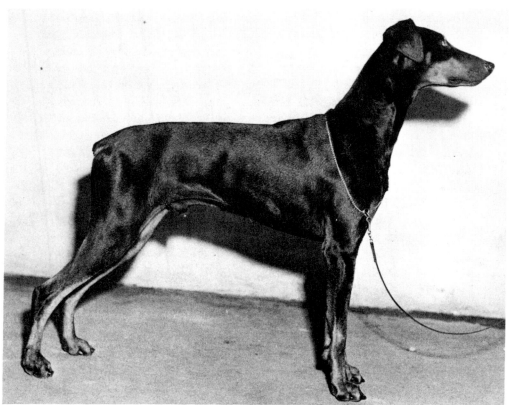

the front and side, are perfectly straight and parallel to each other from elbow to pastern, muscled and sinewy, with round bone proportionate to body structure. In a normal position and when gaiting, the elbow should lie close to the brisket.

BODY: Should be square, height measured vertically from the ground to the highest point of the withers, equalling the length measured horizontally, from the forechest to rear projection of the upper thigh. The back should be short and firm with the topline sloping slightly from the withers to the croup, the female needing room to carry litters may be slightly longer to loin. The belly should be fairly well tucked up. Ribs should be deep and well-sprung, reaching to elbow. Long, weak or roach backs to be discouraged.

HINDQUARTERS: Should be parallel to each other and wide enough apart to fit in with a properly built body. The hip bone should fall away from the spinal column at an angle of about 30 degrees. Croup well filled out. The hindquarters should be well developed and muscular, with long bent stifle and their hocks turning neither in nor out. While the dog is at rest, hock to heel should be perpendicular to the ground.

FEET: Fore-feet should be well arched, compact and cat-like, turning neither in nor out. All dew claws to be removed. Long, flat deviating paws and weak pasterns should be penalised. Hindfeet should be well arched, compact and cat-like, turning neither in nor out.

GAIT: Should be free, balanced and vigorous with good reach in the forequarters, and a driving power in the hindquarters. When trotting, there should be a strong rear-action drive with rotary motion of hindquarters. Rear and front legs should be thrown neither in nor out. Back should remain strong and firm.

TAIL: The tail should be docked at the first or second joint and should appear to be a continuation of the spine, without material drop.

COAT: Should be smooth-haired, short, hard, thick and close lying. Invisible grey undercoat on neck permissible.

COLOUR: Colours allowed are definite black, brown, blue or fawn with rust red markings. Markings must be sharply defined and appearing above each eye and on the muzzle, throat and fore-chest, and on all legs and feet, and below tail. White markings of any kind are highly undesirable.

WEIGHT AND SIZE: Ideal height at withers—Males 27 inches; Females 25½ inches. Considerable deviation from this ideal to be discouraged.

Faults: top drawing, too much slope to croup. Long in loin. Soft in back (swayed). Neck, wet, too short and too thick. Not enough body depth (shallow). Thighs lack width. Lacking in rear angulation. Soft in pastern. Too much stop. Roman nose. Bottom drawing, roach-backed. Tail cropped too long. Shoulders too far forward and lacking in skeletal angulation. Feet soft and thin. Hindquarters overangulated. Sickle hocks. Lacking in bone. Drawing by Ernest Hart.

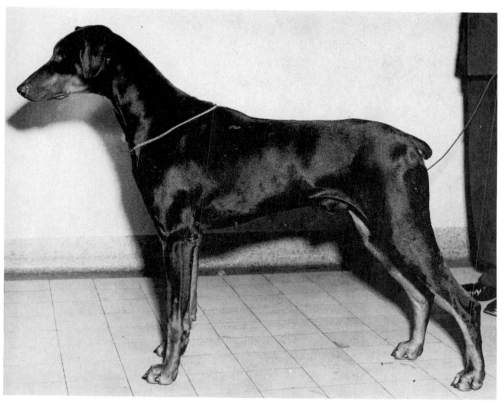

English Ch. Acclimation of Tavey, owned by Mrs. J. Curnow.

FAULTS: Shyness or viciousness must be heavily penalised. Head out of balance in proportion to body, dish-faced, snipy or cheeky should be penalised. Light eyes in black dogs to be discouraged. Overshot or undershot mouths, badly arranged or decayed teeth to be penalised. Dewlap and loose skin are undesirable. Long, weak or roach backs to be discouraged. White markings of any kind are highly undesirable. Hair forming a ridge on the back of the neck and/or along the spine should be classed as a serious fault.

NOTE: Male animals should have two apparently normal testicles fully descended into the scrotum.

Glenayre Jamison and friend Christian. Owned by Jay-Mee's Dobbies, San Juan, Puerto Rico.

Chapter 7

The Doberman as a Family Member

We have read a great deal about the heroic deeds of Dobermans: their catching and holding of criminals; their cutting down on robberies as they police department stores at night; their protecting master and property as they accompany watchmen on their rounds; their finding lost children by following a trail. You name it, and if it takes canine brains, power, loyalty, and fearlessness, a Doberman very likely can handle the situation.

The true unsung heroes, however, are the family dogs, the dogs who share our lives and households, bringing pleasure, love, and security; who love and protect our children; who are content just being with us. It is excellence in these areas that lead a breed to popularity with the public and that are largely accountable for the steady rise in annual registrations of the Doberman Pinscher.

The Doberman is the family dog par excellence: hardy, strong, sensible, intelligent, and beautiful! Here is a dog of whom to be proud, whether he is at home where he behaves in a thoroughly gentlemanly manner; traveling with you, where he is pleasant, protective company; walking with you, which he does staying quietly by your side; playing with your children, which he can do happily hours on end; or gracing your country estate or being content in your city apartment. You will be amazed at his intelligence as he matures, for Dobermans often truly seem to read our thoughts; the accuracy with which he senses danger, for he almost knows instinctively what are and are not situations to be watched or investigated; and the adaptability with which he adjusts his

55

Toni Leigh Di Nardo, daughter of Dr. and Mrs. Anthony Di Nardo, with a handsome Lone Eagle daughter. All of the Di Nardo kids are great dog show enthusiasts; all have competed successfully in Junior Showmanship.

own mood to ours, whether it be to relax at our side or accompany us anywhere that he is welcome.

Dobermans thrive nicely under apartment living, so do not be afraid, if you yearn for one, to have him with you there. You will need to provide him with several trips out daily and at least once a day a good walk; but for the rest he can gain sufficient exercise moving freely around the apartment. And after all, no matter what breed or size dog you own, trips out are necessary—and probably safer for you if accompanied by a dog who demands the respect of a Doberman!

If you live in the suburbs or country, you will need to provide a fenced area for the dog (also par for the course no matter what your breed), and, again, it will be necessary to take him for a daily walk to keep him in good muscle and condition. Dogs generally do not gain a great deal of exercise when left in a fenced area, but they can thus *safely* enjoy the outdoor area and the fresh air to keep them healthy. *Never, never, ever*, no matter how far out in the country you may live, permit a dog to run free unless you are there supervising his activities. So many things can happen to a dog thus unprotected that it simply is not worth the risk—or the possible heartache which may result. Only the most uncaring and irresponsible of dog owners ever submit their supposedly much loved pets to the danger of cars, loss, poisoning, traps, being stolen, or any of half a dozen other perils which can lead to complete disaster for the dog. If you do not intend to care for your dog, do not own one!

Dobermans are not quarrelsome by nature, and they seldom start fights with other animals. Should another dog, however, have the poor judgment to start a fight with a Dobe, he will find himself facing a formidable opponent, for a Doberman can more than hold his own.

If you like working with your dog, your Doberman is a "natural" here, too. Join an obedience class with him and first thing you know you may find yourself with the potential holder of a Companion Dog degree (C.D.) which is attained in competition at American Kennel Club obedience trials.

A Doberman is also a fun breed to show, but in order to succeed he must be a really excellent dog; competition in this breed is especially keen with huge entries and many splendid dogs competing. This sort of competition is a true challenge; and if it is for you, get busy and take your dog to training classes, then try some match shows, and see if he is well accepted. Once you have him and yourself trained for good showmanship, go out and try the "big time." Although competition is

Jorob's Sweet Sherry, owned by N. Hughan, Liverpool, England. Winner of many first prizes, four Bests of Breed and a Working Group. Pictured here informally with Mrs. Rita Hughan, England.

very keen in the breed, at least there is no complicated grooming involved as in so many other breeds. It is quite simple, really, to keep your Dobe looking ready to step into the ring provided you keep him in good condition (neither too fat nor too thin, coat clean and glossy, bright-eyed and alert)—which, after all, is the way a well-cared-for pet should look, too.

In the selection of a Doberman, you have chosen one of the world's finest breeds. Respect your dog; take pride in him. Love and enjoy him. You will find your efforts lavishly rewarded.

Ch. Star Dobe's Irish Fantasy out for a ride with her handler Bob Hastings. Owned by Don Gau, Honolulu, Hawaii.

Doberman puppy from the kennels of Mrs. V.T. Cuthbertson, Cottage Farm, Huntington, Cambs, in England.

Chapter 8

The Purchase of Your Dog or Puppy

Careful consideration should be given to what breed of dog you wish to own prior to your purchase of one. If several breeds are attractive to you, and you are undecided which you prefer, learn all you can about the characteristics of each before making your decision. As you do so, you are thus preparing yourself to make an intelligent choice; and this is very important when buying a dog who will be, with reasonable luck, a member of your household for at least a dozen years or more. Obviously since you are reading this book, you have decided on the breed—so now all that remains is to make a good choice.

It is never wise to just rush out and buy the first cute puppy who catches your eye. Whether you wish a dog to show, one with whom to compete in obedience, or one as a family dog purely for his (or her) companionship, the more time and thought you invest as you plan the purchase, the more likely you are to meet with complete satisfaction. The background and early care behind your pet will reflect in the dog's future health and temperament. Even if you are planning the purchase purely as a pet, with no thoughts of showing or breeding in the dog's or puppy's future, it is essential that if the dog is to enjoy a trouble-free future you assure yourself of a healthy, properly raised puppy or adult from sturdy, well-bred stock.

Throughout the pages of this book you will find the names of many well-known and well-established kennels in various areas. Another source of information is the American Kennel Club (51 Madison Avenue, New York, NY 10010) from whom you can obtain a list of

Australian Ch. Stehle Binda at fourteen months after winning at Victoria in 1982. Owned by A. Eschbach, North Wagga, Australia.

"We want dinner, please!" is what these Dobe puppies seem to be saying. Owned by J. and G. Joffe, Ft. Lauderdale, Florida.

This handsome uncropped Doberman is Australian Ch. Stehle von Wickens at nine months of age. A splendid representative of the noted Australian Kennel whose name he carries.

63

recognized breeders in the vicinity of your home. If you plan to have your dog campaigned by a professional handler, by all means let the handler help you locate and select a good dog. Through their numerous clients, handlers have access to a variety of interesting show prospects; and the usual arrangement is that the handler re-sells the dog to you for what his cost has been, with the agreement that the dog be campaigned for you by him throughout the dog's career. It is strongly recommended that prospective purchasers follow these suggestions, as you thus will be better able to locate and select a satisfactory puppy or dog.

Your first step in searching for your puppy is to make appointments at kennels specializing in the chosen breed, where you can visit and inspect the dogs, both those available for sale and the kennel's basic breeding stock. You are looking for an active, sturdy puppy with bright eyes and intelligent expression and who is friendly and alert; avoid puppies who are hyperactive, dull, or listless. The coat should be clean and thick, with no sign of parasites. The premises on which he was raised should look (and smell) clean and be tidy, making it obvious that the puppies and their surroundings are in capable hands. Should the kennels featuring the breed you intend owning be sparse in your area or not have what you consider attractive, do not hesitate to contact others at a distance and purchase from them if they seem better able to supply a puppy or dog who will please you *so long as it is a recognized breeding kennel of that breed.* Shipping dogs is a regular practice nowadays, with comparatively few problems when one considers the number of dogs shipped each year. A reputable, well-known breeder wants the customer to be satisfied; thus he will represent the puppy fairly. Should you not be pleased with the puppy upon arrival, a breeder such as has been described will almost certainly permit its return. A conscientious breeder takes real interest and concern in the welfare of the dogs he or she causes to be brought into the world. Such a breeder also is proud of a reputation for integrity. Thus on two counts, for the sake of the dog's future and the breeder's reputation, to such a person a *satisfied* customer takes precedence over a sale at any cost.

If your puppy is to be a pet or "family dog," the earlier the age at which it joins your household the better. Puppies are weaned and ready to start out on their own, under the care of a sensible new owner, at about six weeks old; and if you take a young one, it is often easier to train it to the routine of your household and your requirements of it than is the case with an older dog which, even though still a

Alou Bo Brummel de Baviere, owned by Diane and Robert Dubois, winning first in the Puppy Working Group and second in the regular Working Group under Robert S. Forsyth at eight months old in 1983. A nice representative of Canadian Dobermans.

puppy technically, may have already started habits you will find difficult to change. The younger puppy is usually less costly, too, as it stands to reason the breeder will not have as much expense invested in it. Obviously, a puppy that has been raised to five or six months old represents more in care and cash expenditure on the breeder's part than one sold earlier and therefore should be and generally is priced accordingly.

There is an enormous amount of truth in the statement that "bargain" puppies seldom turn out to be that. A "cheap" puppy, cheaply raised purely for sale and profit, can and often does lead to great heartbreak including problems and veterinarian's bills which can add up to many times the initial cost of a properly reared dog. On the other hand, just because a puppy is expensive does not assure one that is healthy and well reared. There have been numerous cases where unscrupulous dealers have sold for several hundred dollars puppies that were sickly, in poor condition, and such poor specimens that the breed of which they were supposedly members was barely recognizable. So one cannot always judge a puppy by price alone. Common sense must guide a prospective purchaser, plus the selection of a *reliable*, well-recommended dealer whom you know to have well-satisfied customers or, best of all, a specialized breeder. You will probably find the fairest pricing at the kennel of a breeder. Such a person, experienced with the breed in general and with his or her own stock in particular, through extensive association with these dogs has watched enough of them mature to have obviously learned to assess quite accurately each puppy's potential—something impossible where such background is non-existent.

One more word on the subject of pets. Bitches make a fine choice for this purpose as they are usually quieter and more gentle than the males, easier to house train, more affectionate, and less inclined to roam. If you do select a bitch and have no intention of breeding or showing her, by all means have her spayed, for your sake and for hers. The advantages to the owner of a spayed bitch include avoiding the nuisance of "in season" periods which normally occur twice yearly, with the accompanying eager canine swains haunting your premises in an effort to get close to your female, plus the unavoidable messiness and spotting of furniture and rugs at this time, which can be annoying if she is a household companion in the habit of sharing your sofa or bed. As for the spayed bitch, she benefits as she grows older because this simple operation almost entirely eliminates the possibility of breast cancer ever occurring. We believe that all bitches should eventually be spayed—even those used for show or breeding when their careers are ended—in order that they may enjoy a happier, healthier old age. Please take note, however, that a bitch who has been spayed (or an altered dog) *cannot be shown at American Kennel Club Dog shows once this operation has been performed.* Be certain that you are *not* interested in showing her before taking this step.

Also in selecting a pet, never underestimate the advantages of an older dog, perhaps a retired show dog or a bitch no longer needed for breeding, who may be available quite reasonably priced by a breeder anxious to place such a dog in a loving home. These dogs are settled and can be a delight to own, as they make wonderful companions, especially in a household of adults where raising a puppy can sometimes be a trial.

Everything we have said about careful selection of your pet puppy and its place of purchase applies, but with many further considerations, when you plan to buy a show dog or foundation stock for a future breeding program. Now is the time for an in-depth study of the breed, starting with every word and every illustration in this book and all others you can find written on the subject. The standard of the breed now has become your guide, and you must learn not only the words but also how to interpret them and how they are applicable in actual dogs before you are ready to make an intelligent selection of a show dog.

If you are thinking in terms of a dog to show, obviously you must have learned about dog shows and must be in the habit of attending them. This is fine, but now your activity in this direction should be increased, with your attending every single dog show within a reasonable distance from your home. Much can be learned about a breed at ringside at these events. Talk with the breeders who are exhibiting. Study the dogs they are showing. Watch the judging with concentration, noting each decision made and attempt to follow the reasoning by which the judge has reached it. Note carefully the attributes of the dogs who win and, for your later use, the manner in which each is presented. Close your ears to the ringside know-it-alls, usually novice owners of only a dog or two and very new to the fancy, who have only derogatory remarks to make about all that is taking place unless they happen to win. This is the type of exhibitor who "comes and goes" through the fancy and whose interest is usually of very short duration owing to lack of knowledge and dissatisfaction caused by the failure to recognize the need to learn. You, as a fancier who we hope will last

Tolane's Zoe v Zenodobe, double grandaughter of Ch. Zenodobe's Arius, born in February 1982, owned and handled by Nancy H. Woods, Boothbay, Maine. Winning Best of Breed here under Robert S. Forsyth en route to Group 3rd judged by Ernest Loeb.

Opposite page: Harcox Lincoln at 18 months. A double grandson of Eng. Ch. Olderhill Sheboygen, his wins have included a Reserve Best Puppy in Show when eight and a half months old. Miss Lesley Wright, owner, Margate, Kent, England.

and enjoy our sport over many future years, should develop independent thinking at this stage; you should learn to draw your own conclusions about the merits, or lack of them, seen before you in the ring and thus, sharpen your own judgment in preparation for choosing wisely and well.

Note carefully which breeders campaign winning dogs, not just an occasional isolated good one but consistent, homebred winners. It is from one of these people that you should select your own future "star."

If you are located in an area where dog shows take place only occasionally or where there are long travel distances involved, you will need to find another testing ground for your ability to select a worthy show dog. Possibly, there are some representative kennels raising this breed within a reasonable distance. If so, by all means ask permission of the owners to visit the kennels and do so when permission is granted. You may not necessarily buy then and there, as they may not have available what you are seeking that very day, but you will be able to see the type of dog being raised there and to discuss the dogs with the breeder. Every time you do this, you add to your knowledge. Should one of these kennels have dogs which especially appeal to you, perhaps you could reserve a show-prospect puppy from a coming litter. This is frequently done, and it is often worth waiting for a puppy, unless you have seen a dog with which you are truly greatly impressed and which is immediately available.

We have already discussed the purchase of a pet puppy. Obviously this same approach applies in a far greater degree when the purchase involved is a future show dog. The only place at which to purchase a show prospect is from a breeder who raises show-type stock; otherwise, you are almost certainly doomed to disappointment as the puppy matures. Show and breeding kennels obviously cannot keep all of their fine young stock. An active breeder-exhibitor is, therefore, happy to place promising youngsters in the hands of people also interested in showing and winning with them, doing so at a fair price according to the quality and prospects of the dog involved. Here again, if no kennel in your immediate area has what you are seeking, do not hesitate to contact top breeders in other areas and to buy at long distance. Ask for pictures, pedigrees, and a complete description. Heed the breeder's advice and recommendations, after truthfully telling exactly what your expectations are for the dog you purchase. Do you want something with which to win just a few ribbons now and then? Do you want a dog who can complete his championship? Are you thinking of the real "big time" (*i.e.,* seriously campaigning with Best of Breed, Group wins, and possibly even Best in Show as your eventual goal)? Consider it all carefully in advance; then honestly discuss your plans with the breeder. You will be better satisfied with the results if you do this, as the breeder is then in the best position to help you choose the dog who is most likely to come through for you. A breeder selling a show dog is just as anxious as the buyer for the dog to succeed, and the breeder will represent the dog to you with truth and honesty. Also, this type of breeder does not lose interest the moment the sale has been made but when necessary will be right there ready to assist you with beneficial advice and suggestions based on years of experience.

As you make inquiries of at least several kennels, keep in mind that show-prospect puppies are less expensive than mature show dogs, the latter often costing close to four figures, and sometimes more. The reason for this is that, with a puppy, there is always an element of chance, the possibility of its developing unexpected faults as it matures or failing to develop the excellence and quality that earlier had seemed probable. There definitely is a risk factor in buying a show-prospect puppy. Sometimes all goes well, but occasionally the swan becomes an ugly duckling. Reflect on this as you consider available puppies and young adults. It just might be a good idea to go with a more mature, though more costly, dog if one you like is available.

When you buy a mature show dog, "what you see is what you get"; and it is not likely to change beyond coat and condition which are dependent on your care. Also advantageous for a novice owner is the fact that a mature dog of show quality almost certainly will have received show ring training and probably match show experience, which will make your earliest handling ventures far easier.

Frequently it is possible to purchase a beautiful dog who has completed championship but who, owing to similarity in bloodlines, is not needed for the breeder's future program. Here you have the opportunity of owning a champion, usually in the two- to five-year-old range, which you can enjoy campaigning as a Special (for Best of Breed competition) and which will be a settled, handsome dog for you and your family to enjoy with pride.

If you are planning foundation for a future kennel, concentrate on acquiring one or two really superior bitches. These need not necessarily be top show-quality, but they should represent your breed's finest producing bloodlines from a strain noted for producing quality, generation after generation. A proven matron who is already the dam

Ch. Eagle's Devil "D", a sensational puppy who matured into a very successful Best in Show and record-holding dog, pictured here in his early days with then-handler Jane Forsyth. The Forsyths have now turned from handling to judging, and Devil's career is now in the capable hands of Carlos Rojas. Owned by Dr. and Mrs. Anthony Di Nardo.

A very handsome Doberman from Canada. Ch. Ryas Anticipation at two and a half years of age, owned by Pat Cunningham, Vinemount, Ontario.

Ch. Mikadobe Valentino v Paris finishing here under judge A.K. Nicholas, at Columbus K.C. in December 1980. Owners are Mr. Kuzo Sasada of Japan and Mae Downey of the United States. Handled by Carlos Rojas, bred by Carlos and Kathy Rojas.

of show-type puppies is, of course, the ideal selection; but these are usually difficult to obtain, no one being anxious to part with so valuable an asset. You just might strike it lucky, though, in which case you are off to a flying start. If you cannot find such a matron available, select a young bitch of finest background from top producing lines who is herself of decent type, free of obvious faults, and of good quality.

Great attention should be paid to the pedigree of the bitch from whom you intend to breed. If not already known to you, try to see the sire and dam. It is generally agreed that someone starting with a breed should concentrate on a fine collection of top-flight bitches and raise a few litters from these before considering keeping one's own stud dog. The practice of buying a stud and then breeding everything you own or acquire to that dog does not always work out well. It is better to take advantage of the many noted sires who are available to be used at stud, who represent all of the leading strains, and in each case carefully to select the one who in type and pedigree seems most compatible to each of your bitches, at least for your first several litters.

To summarize, if you want a "family dog" as a companion, it is best to buy it young and raise it to the habits of your household. If you are buying a show dog, the more mature it is, the more certain you can be of its future beauty. If you are buying foundation stock for a kennel, then bitches are better, but they must be from the finest *producing* bloodlines.

When you buy a pure-bred dog that you are told is eligible for registration with the American Kennel Club, you are entitled to receive from the seller an application form which will enable you to register your dog. If the seller cannot give you the application form you should demand and receive an identification of your dog consisting of the name of the breed, the registered names and numbers of the sire and dam, the name of the breeder, and your dog's date of birth. If the litter of which your dog is a part is already recorded with the American Kennel Club, then the litter number is sufficient identification.

Do not be misled by promises of papers at some later date. Demand a registration application form or proper identification as described above. If neither is supplied, do not buy the dog. So warns the American Kennel Club, and this is especially important in the purchase of show or breeding stock.

Chapter 9

The Care of Your Puppy

Preparing for Your Puppy's Arrival

The moment you decide to be the new owner of a puppy is not one second too soon to start planning for the puppy's arrival in your home. Both the new family member and you will find the transition period easier if your home is geared in advance for the arrival.

The first things to be prepared are a bed for the puppy and a place where you can pen him up for rest periods. We believe that every dog should have a crate of its own from the very beginning, so that he will come to know and love it as his special place where he is safe and happy. It is an ideal arrangement, for when you want him to be free, the crate stays open. At other times you can securely latch it and know that the pup is safely out of mischief. If you travel with him, his crate comes along in the car; and, of course, in traveling by plane there is no alternative but to have a carrier for the dog. If you show your dog, you will want him upon occasion to be in a crate a good deal of the day. So from every consideration, a crate is a very sensible and sound investment in your puppy's future safety and happiness and for your own peace of mind.

The crates we recommend are the wooden ones with removable side panels, which are ideal for cold weather (with the panels in place to keep out drafts) and in hot weather (with the panels removed to allow better air circulation). Wire crates are all right in the summer, but they give no protection from cold or drafts. Aluminum crates are not recommended due to the manner in which aluminum reflects surrounding temperatures. If it is cold, so is the metal of the crate; if it is hot, the crate becomes burning hot. For this reason we consider aluminum crates neither comfortable nor safe.

Ch. Elexa's Final Flair of Selena owned by Shirley McCoy seen here taking Best of Winners at Old Dominion in 1978, handled by Jane Forsyth.

Ch. Vormund's Candy Spots belongs to Howard Aubin and was shown to his title by Jane Forsyth.

When you choose the puppy's crate, be certain that it is roomy enough not to become outgrown. The crate should have sufficient height so the dog can stand up in it as a mature dog and sufficient area so that he can stretch out full length when relaxed. When the puppy is young, first give him shredded newspaper as a bed; the papers can be replaced with a mat or turkish towels when the dog is older. Carpet remnants are great for the bottom of the crate, as they are inexpensive and in case of accidents can be quite easily replaced. As the dog matures and is past the chewing age, a pillow or blanket in the crate is an appreciated comfort.

Sharing importance with the crate is a safe area in which the puppy can exercise and play. If you are an apartment dweller, a baby's playpen for a toy dog or a young puppy works out well; for a larger breed or older puppy use a portable exercise pen which you can then use later when traveling with your dog or for dog shows. If you have a yard, an area where he can be outside in safety should be fenced in prior to the dog's arrival at your home. This area does not need to be huge, but it does need to be made safe and secure. If you are in a suburban area where there are close neighbors, stockade fencing works out best as then the neighbors are less aware of the dog and the dog cannot see and bark at everything passing by. If you are out in the country where no problems with neighbors are likely to occur, then regular chain-link fencing is fine. For added precaution in both cases, use a row of concrete blocks or railroad ties inside against the entire bottom of the fence; this precludes or at least considerably lessens the chances of your dog digging his way out.

Be advised that if yours is a single dog, it is very unlikely that it will get sufficient exercise just sitting in the fenced area, which is what most of them do when they are there alone. Two or more dogs will play and move themselves around, but from my own experience, one by itself does little more than make a leisurely tour once around the area to check things over and then lies down. You must include a daily walk or two in your plans if your puppy is to be rugged and well. Exercise is extremely important to a puppy's muscular development and to keep a mature dog fit and trim. So make sure that those exercise periods, or walks, a game of ball, and other such activities, are part of your daily program as a dog owner.

If your fenced area has an outside gate, provide a padlock and key and a strong fastening for it, and use them, so that the gate can not be opened by others and the dog taken or turned free. The ultimate convenience in this regard is, of course, a door (unused for other purposes) from the house around which the fenced area can be enclosed, so that all you have to do is open the door and out into his area he goes. This arrangement is safest of all, as then you need not be using a gate, and it is easier in bad weather since then you can send the dog out without taking him and becoming soaked yourself at the same time. This is not always possible to manage, but if your house is arranged so that you could do it this way, you would never regret it due to the convenience and added safety thus provided. Fencing in the entire yard, with gates to be opened and closed whenever a caller, deliveryman, postman, or some other person comes on your property, really is not safe at all because people not used to gates and their importance are frequently careless about closing and latching gates *securely*. There have been many heartbreaking incidents brought about by someone carelessly only half closing a gate which the owner had thought to be firmly latched and the dog wandering out. For greatest security a fenced *area* definitely takes precedence over a fenced *yard*.

The puppy will need a collar (one that fits now, not one to be grown into) and lead from the moment you bring him home. Both should be an appropriate weight and type for his size. Also needed are a feeding dish and a water dish, both made preferably of unbreakable material. Your pet supply shop should have an interesting assortment of these and other accessories from which you can choose. Then you will need grooming tools of the type the breeder recommends and some toys. One of the best toys is a beef bone, either rib, leg, or knuckle (the latter the type you can purchase to make soup), cut to an appropriate size for your puppy dog. These are absolutely safe and are great exercise for the teething period, helping to get the baby teeth quickly out of the way with no problems. Equally satisfactory is Nylabone® , a nylon bone that does not chip or splinter and that "frizzles" as the puppy chews, providing healthful gum massage. Rawhide chews are safe, too, *IF made in the United States.* There was a problem a few years back owing to the chemicals with which some foreign rawhide toys had been treated, since which time we have carefully avoided giving them to our own dogs. Also avoid plastics and any sort of rubber toys, *particularly* those with squeakers which the puppy may remove and swallow. If you want a ball for the puppy to use when playing with him, select one of very hard construction made for this purpose and do not leave it alone with him because he may chew off and swallow bits of the rubber. Take the ball with you when the game is over. This also

(*Top*) Kimbertal's Prima Donna owned by Sheridan Pausey's Windswept Kennels, New South Wales, Australia. (*Bottom*) A puppy sent to Hong Kong from Australia owned by Mr. Wong Wing On. Bred by Windswept Kennels.

(*Top*) Ganna's Something Special of Tavey from the Tavey Dobermans, West Sussex, England. (*Bottom*) Tavey's Diploma, a very handsome dog owned by Tavey Dobermans.

applies to some of those "tug of war" type rubber toys which are fun when used with the two of you for that purpose but again should *not* be left behind for the dog to work on with his teeth. Bits of swallowed rubber, squeakers, and other such foreign articles can wreak great havoc in the intestinal tract—do all you can to guard against them.

Too many changes all at once can be difficult for a puppy. For at least the first few days he is with you, keep him on the food and feeding schedule to which he is accustomed. Find out ahead of time from the breeder what he feeds his puppies, how frequently, and at what times of the day. Also find out what, if any, food supplements the breeder has been using and recommends. Then be prepared by getting in a supply of the same food so that you will have it there when you bring the puppy home. Once the puppy is accustomed to his new surroundings, then you can switch the type of food and schedule to fit your convenience, but for the first several days do it as the puppy expects.

Your selection of a veterinarian also should be attended to before the puppy comes home, because you should stop at the vet's office for the puppy to be checked over as soon as you leave the breeder's premises. If the breeder is from your area, ask him for recommendations. Ask your dog-owning friends for their opinions of the local veterinarians, and see what their experiences with those available have been. Choose someone whom several of your friends recommend highly, then contact him about your puppy, perhaps making an appointment to stop in at his office. If the premises are clean, modern, and well equipped, and if you like the veterinarian, make an appointment to bring the puppy in on the day of purchase. Be sure to obtain the puppy's health record from the breeder, including information on such things as shots and worming that the puppy has had.

Joining the Family

Remember that, exciting and happy an occasion as it is for you, the puppy's move from his place of birth to your home can be, for him, a traumatic experience. His mother and littermates will be missed. He quite likely will be awed or frightened by the change of surroundings. The person on whom he depended will be gone. Everything should be planned to make his arrival at your home pleasant—to give him confidence and to help him realize that yours is a pretty nice place to be after all.

Never bring a puppy home on a holiday. There just is too much going on with people and gifts and excitement. If he is in honor of an

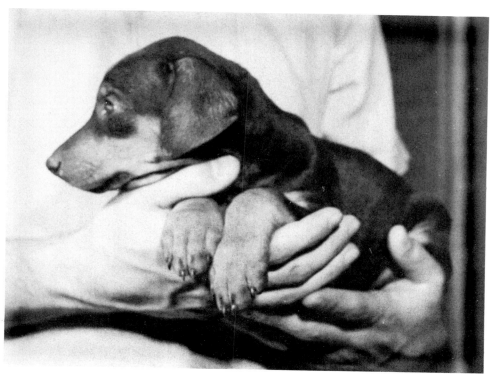

Feeling safe and comfortable, a Doberman puppy held correctly will not struggle to be free.

"occasion," work it out so that his arrival will be a few days earlier or, perhaps even better, a few days later than the "occasion." Then your home will be back to its normal routine and the puppy can enjoy your undivided attention. Try not to bring the puppy home in the evening. Early morning is the ideal time, as then he has the opportunity of getting acquainted and the initial strangeness should wear off before bedtime. You will find it a more peaceful night that way. Allow the puppy to investigate as he likes, under your watchful eye. If you already have a pet in the household, keep a careful watch that the relationship between the two gets off to a friendly start or you may quickly find yourself with a lasting problem. Much of the future attitude of each toward the other will depend on what takes place that first day, so keep your mind on what they are doing and let your other activities slide for the moment. Be careful not to let your older pet become jealous by paying more attention to the puppy than to him, as that will start a bad situation immediately.

Good Luck Fortune O'Liquorish (15 months of age) by Ch. Liquorish Rico's Luck Chance, C.D., R.O.M. ex Apollo's Good Luck Charm, C.D., is owned by S. and F. Trespalacios and G. Joffe, Ft. Lauderdale, Florida.

Opposite page: A lovely portrait of the noted winner Am. and Can. Ch. Star Dobe's Irish Fantasy owned by Don Gau, Honolulu, Hawaii.

If you have a child, here again it is important that the relationship start out well. Before the puppy is brought home, you should have a talk with the youngster about puppies, so that it will be clearly understood that puppies are fragile and can easily be injured; therefore, they should not be teased, hurt, mauled, or overly rough-housed. A puppy is not an inanimate toy; it is a living thing with a right to be loved and handled respectfully, treatment which will reflect in the dog's attitude toward your child as both mature together. Never permit your children's playmates to mishandle the puppy, tormenting the puppy until it turns on the children in self-defense. Children often do not realize how rough is too rough. You, as a responsible adult, are obligated to assure that your puppy's relationship with children is a pleasant one.

Do not start out by spoiling your puppy. A puppy is usually pretty smart and can be quite demanding. What you had considered to be "just for tonight" may be accepted by the puppy as "for keeps." Be firm with him, strike a routine, and stick to it. The puppy will learn more quickly this way, and everyone will be happier at the result. A radio playing softly or a dim night light are often comforting to a puppy as it gets accustomed to new surroundings and should be provided in preference to bringing the puppy to bed with you—unless, of course, you intend him to share the bed as a permanent arrangement.

Feeding Your Dog

Time was when providing nourishing food for our dogs involved a far more complicated procedure than people now feel is necessary. The old school of thought was that the daily ration must consist of fresh beef, vegetables, cereal, egg yolks, and cottage cheese as basics with such additions as brewer's yeast and vitamin tablets on a daily basis.

During recent years, however, many minds have changed regarding this procedure. We still give eggs, cottage cheese, and supplements to the diet, but the basic method of feeding dogs has changed; and the change has been, in the opinion of many authorities, definitely for the better. The school of thought now is that you are doing your dogs a favor when you feed them some of the fine commercially prepared dog foods in preference to your own home-cooked concoctions.

The reason behind this new outlook is easily understandable. The dog food industry has grown to be a major one, participated in by some of the best known and most respected names in the American way of life. These trusted firms, it is agreed, turn out excellent products, so people are feeding their dog food preparations with confidence and the dogs are thriving, living longer, happier, and healthier lives than ever before. What more could we want?

There are at least half a dozen absolutely top-grade dry foods to be mixed with broth or water and served to your dog according to directions. There are all sorts of canned meats, and thére are several kinds of "convenience foods," those in a packet which you open and dump out into the dog's dish. It is just that simple. The "convenience" foods are neat and easy to use when you are away from home, but generally speaking we prefer a dry food mixed with hot water, or soup and meat. We also feel that the canned meat, with its added fortifiers, is more beneficial to the dogs than the fresh meat. However, the two can be alternated or, if you prefer and your dog does well on it, by all means use fresh ground beef. A dog enjoys changes in the meat part of his diet, which is easy with the canned food since all sorts of beef are available (chunk, ground, stewed, and so on), plus lamb, chicken, and even such concoctions as liver and egg, just plain liver flavor, and a blend of five meats.

There also is prepared food geared to every age bracket of your dog's life, from puppyhood on through old age, with special additions or modifications to make it particularly nourishing and beneficial. Our grandparents, and even our parents, never had it so good where the canine dinner is concerned, because these commercially prepared foods are tasty and geared to meeting the dog's gastronomic approval.

Additionally, contents and nutrients are clearly listed on the labels, as are careful instructions for feeding just the right amount for the size, weight, and age of each dog.

With these foods we do not feel the addition of extra vitamins is necessary, but if you do there are several kinds of those, too, that serve as taste treats as well as being beneficial. Your pet supplier has a full array of them.

Of course there is no reason not to cook up something for your dog if you would feel happier doing so. But it seems to us unnecessary when such truly satisfactory rations are available with so much less trouble and expense.

How often you feed your dog is a matter of how it works out best for you. Many owners prefer to do it once a day. Many other owners think that two meals, each of smaller quantity, are better for the digestion and more satisfying to the dog, particularly if yours is a household member who stands around and watches preparations for the family

Ch. Barchet Fiddler On The Roof made a big winning record for Mrs. Alan Robson handled by Terry Lazzaro during the early 1980's. An excellent dog of tremendous quality.

Opposite page: This lovely bitch is Ch. Tara's Scarlet Prima Donna, taking Winners Bitch, Best of Winners, and Best of Opposite Sex at Brevard Kennel Club in 1981. Carol A. Kepler, owner-handler, Sarasota, Florida.

This well-constructed Doberman Pinscher kennel is landscaped with shrubs and trees and cleaned regularly to keep the premises sanitary and attractive.

meals. Do not overfeed. That is the shortest route to all sorts of problems. Follow directions and note carefully how your dog is looking. If your dog is overweight, cut back the quantity of food a bit. If the dog looks thin, then increase the amount. Each dog is an individual and the food intake should be adjusted to his requirements to keep him feeling and looking trim and in top condition.

From the time puppies are fully weaned until they are about twelve weeks old, they should be fed four times daily. From three months to six months of age, three meals should suffice. At six months of age the puppies can be fed two meals, and the twice daily feedings can be continued until the puppies are close to one year old, at which time feeding can be changed to once daily if desired.

If you do feed just once a day, do so by early afternoon at the latest and give the dog a snack, or biscuit or two, at bedtime.

Remember that plenty of fresh water should always be available to your puppy or dog for drinking. This is of utmost importance to his health.

Kennels, Runs, and Bedding

A man's home is his castle and a dog's home is his kennel. But your dog depends on *you* to provide him with clean comfortable quarters.

The first thing you must do when your dog arrives is to show him where he lives. This may be a spot in the house or a doghouse outside. But it is his own place. And the first rule is that kennels and bedding must be kept clean and dry. Dirty living quarters can harbor many germs and parasites which are passed on to the dog.

When your dog arrives, remember that he is in a strange home, far from his family. You have already decided where he is to stay, indoors or outdoors. Show him his new home, but don't just leave him there and depart, turning off the light or closing the door. He's young, probably frightened, and very lonely. A little love and affection and time for him to get acquainted and sniff about his bed or kennel and he'll settle in fast enough.

If you live in an apartment, he will naturally live indoors. If possible, choose a spot that is convenient to the whole family, where the dog can have some privacy. If you live in a house, you have the option of having an indoor or outdoor pet. Most small dogs should be indoors as they have less resistance to weather changes and extremes. A large, active dog is probably better off outdoors in a comfortable house with a large run. But whatever type of housing you provide for your pet, it must be clean, airy, warm in winter, ventilated in summer, and large enough to accommodate your dog.

When should a dog be outside? Small puppies warmed by their mothers can huddle outside in a kennel in quite cold weather. If it is very cold, of course, they should be inside, especially if they are newborn. Older dogs with thick coats and hardy dispositions can stay outdoors. Indeed, it is dangerous to keep an outdoor dog inside for too long. He will be more susceptible to the cold after that.

Professional Kennels

When you consider a kennel for boarding or hospitalization there are certain factors in kennel construction which you should note, to see if the kennel is satisfactory.

A good kennel is large and airy. The ceiling is high, with good ventilation. The kennel contains pens and sleeping areas adequate for the size dog they accommodate, as well as separate quarters for sick dogs and whelping. Each dog should have his own sleep space, but outdoor pens can be shared for exercise. The kennels should be clean. Some

The big-winning young dog Ch. Pajant's Encore V Rockelle, beautifully illustrating what it takes to be a dog show "star" as he stands perfectly posed and at attention, eyes on his handler Terry Lazzaro. "Corey" is owned by Dot Roberts.

Array Exclusive, C.D. at Greater Clark County Dog Show judged by Robert S. Forsyth. Owned by Beth Wilhite and Judith Bingham.

kennels today use wire-bottomed pens. These have the advantage of being easier to keep clean and less likely to harbor germs. A wire-bottomed pen is made up of two parts: a box for sleeping and an outdoor area for play and exercise. A hinged door provides room to clean and show the dogs. Contrary to what many people think, the wire bottom does not injure the dog's feet.

Outdoor Kennels

Most people, however, are concerned with housing a single dog, or two at the most. Outdoor housing can be purchased. If you do buy a doghouse, be sure it is solidly constructed, easy to clean, and adequately ventilated. It must be large enough! A small puppy may grow into a large dog. Veterinarians recommend that the sleeping area, your dog's bedroom, be at least two times the width of the grown dog and one and one-half times his height.

Place the kennel in a spot that has some shade as well as sun. If the roof is hinged, you can open it to air the kennel. If possible, place the house a couple of inches off the ground so that moisture and rodents do not affect your dog.

A Doberman will enjoy chewing on a Nylabone® anytime, but this is needed most of all when he is in a crate or kennel alone.

Be sure that your Doberman's portable kennel or crate is not painted with a lead base paint.

A homemade kennel can be constructed using old lumber and materials from your workshop. Your doghouse should follow the two-room plan: one room for sleeping and an entry way. A porch is nice also, so your dog can watch the world go by without having to lie on wet ground. If you live in a cold climate, the kennel should be insulated. The hinged roof makes it easy to clean.

CAUTION! WHEN YOU PAINT YOUR DOG HOUSE, BE SURE THAT THE PAINT DOES NOT HAVE A LEAD BASE.

Better ventilation will be provided if you slant the roof. And you can also provide a slightly raised curbing at the entry of the bedroom, to keep bedding in place.

To keep the kennel clean, scrub it with hot water. A mild disinfectant can be used to disinfect the kennel. Your dog is proud of his home and not likely to mess it up; but if he has been sick or just wormed, be sure that the kennel is thoroughly scrubbed and disinfected and that the bedding is burned.

The best type of bedding for an outdoor kennel is cedar shavings. Cedar shavings are easily purchased in any pet store, and they smell sweet and clean. Be sure to change the bedding every so often.

Ch. Zeitlin's Rogue Force v Kerri taking Best of Breed at Grand Rapids in May 1982. Dr. A.B. Zeitlin, owner, Highland Park, Illinois. Handled by Jim Berger.

Opposite page: Ch. Barchet Fiddler On The Roof in show pose, baiting perfectly for his handler Terry Lazzaro. This dog is a very famous Group and Best in Show winner who was owned at this time by Mrs. Alan Robson.

Indoor Sleeping Quarters

A dog raised indoors should also have a private place. Sometimes, this may be in the cellar, but this is all right only if you are fortunate enough to have a warm dry cellar. Many people use the family room.

Most people who provide for their dogs indoors purchase a bed. A trip to the neighborhood pet stores will show the number of commercially available sizes and styles. The two major types are wicker and metal, and which one you choose depends on where you plan to put your dog's bed. If he is to be in the kitchen, bedroom, or the family room, the wicker is more attractive. If appearance is no concern, the metal is considered sturdier. Be sure that the metal is painted with a paint which does not have a lead base. If you are worried about your puppy chewing up the wicker and getting splinters, there is a harmless, bitter-tasting preparation on the market which can be rubbed on the wicker and will discourage chewing.

Two types of filling are used for mattresses: cedar shavings and cotton. The mattresses with cedar shavings can be changed, which may be necessary if you have a small puppy. It may be better, while the dog is young, to provide him with an old blanket. But beware—many dogs become attached to their blanket and won't give it up.

Runs

If you have a city dog, you naturally will take him for walks on a leash. Both master and dog can get their daily constitutional this way. But in the suburbs or country, the best way to exercise your dog is to provide a run for him. One of the problems of the country dog is road safety. Since it is possible to run free—either singly or with groups of other dogs—speeding motorists, wild animals, and other natural accidents can endanger his life. The considerate dog owner will provide a place for his dog to exercise when he can't take him out on the leash. The run should be rectangular in shape and as large as possible, up to 20 x 40'. Provide a strong wire fence at least 4' high, with a gate fastened with a spring hook. If there is no wooden or iron top rail, the dog will be less likely to try to jump over. Dogs usually aim at something when they jump; and if there is only a thin strand of wire at the top, he will have no target. The use of tie-out stakes is also to be recommended.

There are many opinions as to the best flooring for runs and kennels. The one basic principle on which all agree is that the material should be easy to keep clean. Some experts recommend concrete, smoothly troweled and finished. Others say that this harbors worm

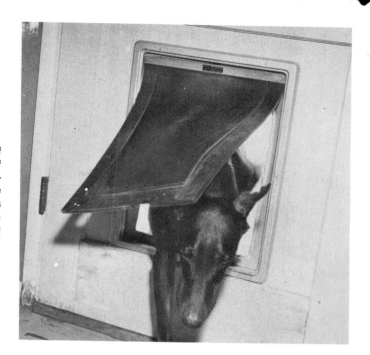

Shown is one of the many kinds of dog doors available. They are manufactured in a variety of models suitable to the breed and size of dog.

eggs and is very hard to keep clean. Sand is often recommended, but the same argument is used against sand. Grass, if your run is not permanent, is satisfactory, but you must expect that it will be considerably trampled.

Some dog owners have the kennel and run together. Others put the dog in the run only for exercise. Protect your dog from the hot sun by providing some shade if there is no doghouse. You can place the run near or under some trees, or construct a platform for protection.

Be sure you provide water also. There is nothing like a fresh drink to cool a fellow off after a hot run around the exercise area. If you do have a run, no matter how large it is, don't leave your pet in it for very long stretches. Dogs, like people, get bored and your dog likes a change of scenery, even if he only goes into the house or his kennel.

The major points to remember about housing and runs are that they must be clean and comfortable. This will keep your dog healthier and happier also.

Ch. Red Sun's Arabasque owned by Gilbert and Lois Bohlin, handled by Jane Forsyth.

Opposite page: (*Top*) Cara's Mandi de Scudamore handled by Terry Lazzaro taking Best of Winners at Long Island K.C. in 1979. (*Bottom*) Ch. Zenodobe's Arius is a lovely BLUE double Zeno grandson. Bred, owned and shown by Nancy H. Woods, Zenodobe Kennels, Boothbay, Maine.

Bunny Lanning of Murray, Kentucky, owns this handsome and talented Doberman, Champion Lothlorien's High-Elven Rune, C.D.X., ROM, who has won many honors in both obedience and show competition. A marvelous example of Doberman versatility, Rune moved easily from the show ring to Junior Showmanship to obedience to Schutzhund training for protection work and to gain certification as a Therapy Dog. A very lovely and admirable example of the Doberman!

Chapter 10

Training Your Doberman

Principles of Training

In today's world of fast-moving cars and crowded cities and suburbs, the life of a dog is truly a *dog's life* if he is improperly trained. The many hazards of living mean the survival of the fittest—and to be fit for today's world a dog must be properly trained to obey his master (or mistress).

The methods are standard with dog trainers—positive training which relies on encouragement and reward, either by praise from the trainer or food, and negative training where mistakes are punished. Combinations of these methods are common.

With either reward or punishment, animal training requires that each step be taught slowly and completely before the next step is introduced. Rewards (positive training) can be *praise* by tone of voice and petting or *food* such as a favorite tidbit, dog candy, or biscuits.

The authors believe that the best and most enduring type of training is positive training, using only the master's voice in praise. Dogs trained with candy or other foods come to rely on this rather than on the person making the command. Of course, this does not mean that you should not occasionally reward your obedient dog with a bit of his favorite food. In extreme cases, you may have to use punitive measures once in a while to convince him of the error of his ways, but this should not be the standard training method for your dog.

Dogs trained negatively with punishment—and some trainers advocate switches or chains thrown near the dogs, paper, or hitting—may become vicious. By and large, most dogs respond to violence in kind. Dogs are not born vicious; they are made so. The uncontrollable dog could have been saved by thoughtful training work when he was

H. ALISATON GALLORETTE W.O.C.

BEST OF
WINNERS

Tuxedo K.C.
ROBERT PHOTO
Sept. 1978

owner: JANET 79. SIMMONS

Ch. Rosecroft The Victorian finished title in September 1978. Handled by Jane Forsyth for owners Sam and Pat Glunt, Carlisle, Pennsylvania.

Opposite page (*Top*) This adorable Dobe puppy is Simca's Blind Faith owned by the Simca Dobermans, Nobleton, Ontario, Canada. (*Bottom*) Ch. Alisaton Gallorette W.A.C. taking Best of Winners at Tuxedo Park in 1978. Handled by Terry Lazzaro. Owned by Janet M. Skidmore.

Above and opposite page: Here is the great European winner Danica Stann's Juon, champion in many countries, giving an example of his working abilities. Owned by the Muleros, noted French fanciers of Dobermans.

young or less wild. Sadly, in most cases, the dog who is mean or wild has to be destroyed or is killed as a result of his foolhardy actions.

There are two types of training your dog can have—*general training* which makes it possible for him to live with the family in peace and *specialized training* to qualify for the A.K.C. obedience trials. Of course, you can also teach your dogs many tricks such as playing dead or begging, for your own enjoyment. Hunting dogs, police and army dogs, and other working breeds need special training. It is most often taught by experts in the field rather than by lay persons.

Ch. Star Dobe's Irish Fantasy winning the Working Group under Lee Reasin at Mt. Ogden K.C. Owned by Don Gau, Honolulu, Hawaii. Handler Bob Hastings.

Ch. Wynterwind's Sierra Shadow, by Ch. Elexa's Final Flair of Selena ex Ch. Wynterwynd's Rusti Nail winning the awards for 1st 9-12 Month Black Puppy Bitch, Best 9-12 Month Puppy and Reserve Futurity Winner, 1982 Doberman Pinscher Club of America Specialty. Jane Forsyth judging. Gene Haupt handler. A. Lanier and V.D. Fouke owners, Pacifica, California.

Never punish your puppy physically if he fails to use the paper you provided. A reprimand uttered in a forceful tone will be sufficient.

When you begin training remember the following: Your puppy is anxious to obey you and is really trying hard even if he doesn't quite succeed at first. Every ounce of puppy love wants to please you. If he can't quite make it the first time, be *patient*. He will make the grade in time when his muscles are all working properly and he has mastered the first steps. Be *consistent*. Use the same word for the same command, and react the same way to his success or lack of success. Don't laugh at something he does one time and then punish him for it the next. Use your *voice*, not your hand, to punish. Very little can be accomplished by beating a dog except to frighten him.

Teach your dog *one step at a time.* He can't learn the more complicated actions until he has mastered the elementary ones. *Reward* your dog immediately if he does it right. Although you can use a treat, we believe that by complimenting your dog and showing him with your voice and mannerisms what a wonderful dog he is, how marvelously well he has learned to sit and how pleased everyone is with him, that he will answer with just oodles of love and willingness to learn more. *Punish* your dog if he refuses or disregards your commands by speaking angrily to him and making him realize that you are displeased; do not use violence or withhold basic necessities such as food.

Housebreaking

Do you have a new puppy? Or has one of the litter remained behind? The very first training you will have to start is *housebreaking*. This is imperative if everyone is to live together harmoniously and in clean quarters. But puppies, like children, cannot be completely trained until they are more mature physically. When you hear of a toilet-trained child of nine months, you can be sure that his mother is trained, not the baby. And so it is with dogs. Most dogs cannot be completely and reliably housebroken until four months of age, when the bladder and anus are under control. This is no cause for despair, however; there is plenty you can do until then to keep the house and your dog's quarters clean.

Most dogs are first paper-broken, unless they live outdoors. A dog will not deliberately mess his bed, but he will look around for a convenient corner. The first thing you must do with a young puppy is to confine him to a fairly small space and cover that space with newspaper. Then he can mess to his heart's content.

If you allow your puppy freedom of the house, you are asking for trouble. But if he does get out and make a puddle right in the middle of the floor, be sure to wipe it up thoroughly. Use a special odor eliminator to remove the odor, or your dog will make a beeline for that spot the minute he escapes again. Once he is trained, you can gradually allow him the run of the house, but keep an eye on him for danger signs.

Dogs instinctively use the same place over and over again. Observe which corner he calls his own, and gradually begin removing the paper until only that spot is covered. Leave a bit of soiled paper there so that the odor will attract him back. Praise him lavishly if he continues to use the spot. Be sure he knows that you are terribly pleased that he has been such a good dog. Of course, he probably won't know what it's all about for a while, but that's all right; he loves it anyway. Dog scents are available at most pet shops to aid you in training your dog should you prefer a more sanitary training method.

As your dog grows up a bit, you will notice that he has to eliminate less and less. Mostly he goes right after naps, meals, or play. Now is the time to start housebreaking. Those people who live in apartments have a more difficult job. They must note the signs, pick up the dog, rush to the elevator or stairs and race outside to the nearest curb, trying to attach the leash and desperately hoping the dog won't wet in some embarrassing place like the elevator. If you live in a house or garden apartment, your job is considerably easier. As soon as you observe the dog beginning to sniff around or go in circles, grab him

Ch. Deviltree's Black Shaft, important Best in Show winner of the mid-70's, with his handler Jeffrey Brucker and judge A.K. Nicholas. This splendid Dobe belongs to Kay Smith.

and head for the outdoors. Be sure to praise and pat him generously when he cooperates. If you lead him to the same spot each day, the odor will remind him of his job. It's amazing how quickly your dog will learn what all these mad dashes outside mean and obey you willingly. Besides, he generally has to go! This does make it easier. There will be lapses occasionally. If your dog wets the rug or messes the kitchen floor, immediately chastise him with your voice. Let him know how ashamed you are and how disgusted you feel. Never hit him, never rub his nose in his own mess, and never wait an hour or so before punishment. Dogs have short memories when they are young, and even fifteen minutes later he won't have the least idea what you are talking about. If the lapse is just temporary, you are in luck. Occasionally you may have to begin again. This sounds discouraging, but it is the only way to housebreak him properly.

The following hints may be helpful:

1. Remember that your small puppy has to go quite frequently, and you should be prepared to take him out. You must plan to be home while this basic training is completed.
2. Remember to take him out after naps, meals, play, or any excitement (such as strangers in the house or other dogs).
3. Praise your dog when he cooperates. Use your voice only when he forgets. And don't expect him to learn the day you begin. Training takes time and the dog must be physically mature.
4. If you let your puppy roam the house, you are asking for trouble; keep him confined to one room until you are absolutely sure.

Early Training

Come

This command should be the first actual training you give your dog aside from housebreaking, and it is the most important. Once your dog learns to come when you call, he is safe from many dangers and is more easily handled.

A puppy should not be forced, so the easiest way to begin training him to come is to begin while he is in the house. Just coax him to you, saying "**Come**" in your most wheedling voice. If there is no other big attraction—such as dinner or strangers—to whom should he come but to you? Who else is so willing to play and means warm food and affection? He will sidle up at the sound of your voice, just begging for a pat. And of course you give him one. Repeat this several times a day, using only the one word "**Come**." Do not keep the lesson up for long and don't punish if he does not obey. Try again, perhaps with a bit of food. When he obeys fairly well, try it outside. Select a quiet spot and call "**Come**." If he refuses to come to you, take courage in hand and run off. You may fear you will lose him, but no puppy can refuse a good chase with his master. If you look around you will see him manfully trying to catch up with you. When he does come up, praise him, pet him, make a big fuss, and don't scold him for not obeying immediately.

Once your dog has begun to catch on to the new word in his vocabulary, you can begin adding his name, so he gets used to that. "Come, Kippy" and then "Kippy, come" will teach him his rightful name.

No and Stop

About the same time as you begin teaching your puppy to come to you, you will probably find yourself telling him "**No**" or "**Stop**." He's in and out of mischief, and you are spending your days trailing him around to see that he isn't puddling as well as keeping him from chewing up the furniture and turning over the garbage can. If he does get into something he shouldn't, shout a loud "**No**" or "**Stop**" and then take him away firmly. If he's bent on chewing, give him something safe to chew (a Nylabone® would be great) and confine him to his room. But be sure and practice consistency. What is forbidden one time should also be forbidden the next, or you may find yourself with a very confused puppy. As a rule it isn't enough just to say "**No**," but you must also remove him from the temptation or take the temptation away from him.

"**Stop**" can be used when you want the puppy to stop some activity such as biting, barking, and growling. Often you will have to close his mouth and hold it shut while you chastise him with "**Stop**" and a most sorrowful look.

Lead Training

Your dog is housebroken and almost knows when to come, and you can begin to think about lead (leash) training. Again, you must have time for training. If you have no spare time, perhaps it would be better to arrange for a professional trainer or school. If you plan to do it yourself, then be prepared to allot sufficient time.

The best type of training collar is a choke collar. This is a collar made of chain, with a ring where the lead is fastened. Slip the collar over the dog's head and attach the chain. A choke collar pulls tighter

Ch. Maple Meadow's Fancy Pants belongs to Linda Willhat and was shown to the title by Jane Forsyth.

Opposite page: Ch. Alisaton Damascus, owned by Gwen DeMilta and Peggy Esposito, handled by Terry Lazzaro. A consistent East Coast winner of the late 1970's.

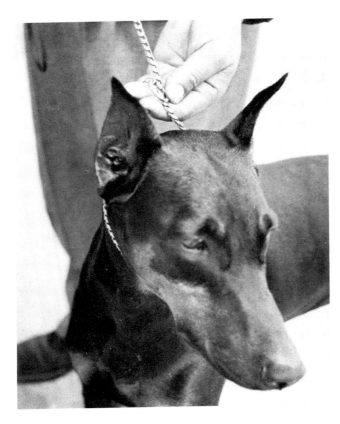

A choke collar is a tried and satisfactory device for training used by many dog owners and professional dog trainers.

when you do, and it loosens when you let up. It should be removed when not in use.

Use a sturdy collar so that it does not harm the dog. The lead can be of leather or chain. Be sure it is strong enough if you have an energetic puppy. When you attach the lead to the collar, have it pass over the dog's neck, not under it.

Suppose you collar your dog, attach the lead, and set out for a pleasant walk with him. The first thing he does is refuse to move. Or perhaps he moves too much, rushing off, and bounding in all directions until brought up by the lead. What now? Obviously, you and this whirling dervish cannot go parading down the street. In the first place, see that you are holding the lead and dog properly. The dog should be on your left side, the lead held in the right hand with your left hand available for extra strength and guidance. If your dog refuses to go with you, take him home. Let him get very hungry; then attach the leash and lead him to his food. If he associates good things with the collar and lead, he will be more cooperative the next time you plan an outing.

Heel

What happens if he rushes off, pulling you along? We have seen any number of people being dragged along by their dogs, and this is surely a sign of poor training. If your puppy runs off, jerk the lead with the left hand and then stop, say "Come," and wait for his return. Praise him when he comes back. Sooner or later your dog will see that his wildness only results in stopping the walk altogether and general disapproval. Don't pull, incidentally; just jerk firmly but not unkindly. If you are full of admiration when he does come back, he will do it more willingly. Pretty soon, you can begin to use the word "Heel" when he comes and walks at your side. If he stops, jerk him back firmly and say "Heel." If he bounds ahead, do the same thing and praise him when he comes back. Before you know it, he will be marching proudly by your side, the perfect gentleman. Of course, be prepared for little mishaps, such as the local cat, another dog, or an auto which may distract your dog before he has thoroughly mastered the commands "Come" and "Heel." Firmness and kindness should prevail, however.

Once you feel that he has thoroughly learned these lessons, try it off the lead.

Hints to Remember

1. Never work with your dog on any lesson until he has relieved himself.
2. Keep the lessons short. Fifteen minutes at a time is plenty.
3. Don't expect a dog to stay at "heel" for the whole walk; after all, he's a dog, isn't he, and a fellow needs a little time to play.

Advanced Training

Sit

Once your dog has learned the aforementioned commands, he is ready for the command "Sit." You begin by adding the word "Down" to his vocabulary. When he comes to you and jumps up, you say "Down" and force him down to the ground. Praise him when he obeys. Keep this up until he has learned not to jump up when you begin training.

The next step is "Sit." Stand the dog on your left side with the lead on, and tell him "Sit." Follow words with action and push his hindquarters down. He may lie down all the way, and then you will just have to haul him up again and push down his hindquarters once more.

Ch. Cabra's Dark and Debonaire, handled by Capt. M.E. Smith for Nina McGrath winning the Working Group in June 1983 under judge Robert S. Forsyth.

Opposite page: This handsome Dobe, Ch. Pajant's Encore v Rockelle is owned by Dot Roberts, New City, New York.

Should he accidentally or actually begin to sit, praise him generously. You can appreciate what a hard lesson this is for him, for all he wants to do is jump up, lap your face, and start playing. Repeat the lesson several times a day for short periods. Don't punish; just reward success or partial success with praise.

The command "Lie down" can be taught in much the same way. Once the lesson is learned, try it without the lead.

Stay

Your dog now comes, heels, sits down, and lies down. But the minute you leave, he does too! If you can teach him to stay, this will prove valuable. Suppose you want him to remain in the car while you shop, or with the baby carriage, or to stay quiet when a friend arrives. He must learn to stay in one place for a short period. Just as with the early lessons, use example and praise. As he learns, increase the scope of the command.

When you first command him to stay, sit him down, say "Stay," and then, holding the leash, walk around him or out toward the end of the lead. Of course, he will jump up and follow you. Don't yell at him; simply walk back and force him back into a sitting position, and then say "Sit—Stay." You can also use a hand signal. Hold the palm of your hand in front of his nose when you say "Sit—Stay." He will learn that as well as the word. After a while, he will get the idea and remain sitting while you walk around him.

When this lesson is learned, you can put the lead on the ground. Perhaps he is again nervous. Hold the lead with your foot. It won't be too long before you can leave him unattended and walk off. If he bolts after you, don't praise him; just repeat the whole lesson again. When you think he is sufficiently trained in the sit-stay position, then try distracting him by running off or bouncing a ball under his nose. Each time, if he gets up and starts off, begin again as before. Once the lesson is over and he has performed well, of course you can pat him and tell him how well he has done. Be careful not to pat him as soon as he has remained sitting for a moment, or he will think that the lesson's over.

The authors believe that if your dog is housebroken and can obey the commands "Come," "Heel," "Sit," "Lie down," and "Stay," he will be completely manageable. You can then teach him tricks if you wish. If you so desire, teach your puppy to beg by propping him in the proper position and encouraging him to repeat this. Do not, however, allow him to use this cute trick to get food from you at the table. If you

Two champion Dobermans owned by Mrs. Dino Di Primio shown in a double heel position.

Nanci Little's Shady Acres Persuasion, U.D.T., WAC, SchH. III, FH, VB, WH, AD, doing a jump with style!

Ch. Bifrost's Zacharian winning the points at Cape Cod in February 1978. Perry Phillips handling for owner Larraine Lemire, Sandwich, Massachussetts.

Ch. Zeitlin's Panther von Kerri owned by Dr. A.B. Zeitlin, Highland Park, Illinois.

A brace of Dobermans in sit position, as seen from the rear.

A Doberman in the process of executing a good broad jump, a requirement in advanced obedience training.

wish to reward him with a dog biscuit or candy at the time of the trick, fine; but if you feed him while you are eating because he begs so cutely, this cute trick will only become an chronic nuisance.

Special Problems

Some dogs, because of indifferent training or lack of training, develop problems which must be cured before they become acute and dangerous. The dog who jumps on people, barks all night, chases cars, and bites or steals food from the table must be retrained.

Jumping on People

There are several ways to combat this. If your dog will not obey your command to get down and not jump, you can try the following: Start by telling him "No" and putting him firmly on the floor. If he stays down, pat him. Some trainers advocate that when the dog jumps up you catch him with your knee so he falls back. This is unpleasant enough to stop him. Don't let him get the idea you are hurting him deliberately. As soon as he obeys, praise him.

Chasing Cars

There is no more dangerous and annoying habit for a dog than chasing cars. Dogs have been hit that way, and often in an effort to avoid the dog the driver endangers the lives of others. The best method is to start early and instill a proper fear of cars. Have another drive a car as you walk your dog along the road. When the car comes along, the driver is to give several loud blasts on the horn. At the same time you jerk your dog over to the side of the road. Repeat this several times, and the dog will instinctively move over to the side when he hears a car.

For the already delinquent dog, more severe methods must be used. The driver of the car can use a water pistol and squirt water at the dog as he jumps out at the car, or the driver can leap out of the car and yell loudly at the dog. Of course, you should be nearby in case the dog becomes frightened enough to attack the man. Once your dog shows that he has learned his lesson, he really deserves a medal! But a piece of dog candy will probably serve just as well.

Barking

Many people purchase a dog for use as a watchdog. Persons on farms or valuable property, or those who are alone at night, may want a dog to warn them of approaching strangers. In these cases, the dog's

(*Top*) Ch. Pajant's Encore v Rockelle at Westminster. Owned by Dot Roberts, New City, New York.

bark is an asset. But the dog who barks all night, barks at everyone regardless of who he is, or never stops barking at familiar people such as the paper boy or trash collector should be trained to be silent. Barking is a dog's way of talking and, of course, you don't want to completely muzzle him. But if you live in an apartment or populous neighborhood, a barking dog is very annoying and he often starts other dogs in the area baying. The resulting night-long chorus can cause troublesome relations with non-dog owners and even some dog owners whose sleep is affected.

Prevention is the best cure, and you can start early after the basic lessons are completed. Begin by leaving your dog alone in his room. If he starts to bark, yell at him or knock loudly at the door. If he persists, go in and look your angriest. You can also be sly and pretend to go away. When he begins to howl, go through the routine again.

Biting

Dogs who bite are potentially dangerous. And dogs who continue to bite can be put away by order of a court if there have been complaints. First and foremost, do not encourage your young puppy to bite people, even playfully (and that is what he is doing when he starts, *just playing*). If he must chew on something, get him some inanimate object such as a toy or a Nylabone® . If he continues to bite, express your disapproval. He may need more severe punishment. Hold his jaw shut until he stops or slap him gently on the muzzle. Be sure to fondle him afterwards if he obeys. If you do not tease your dog, he will be less inclined to bite. A dog doesn't like to be poked or interrupted when he is eating. His instincts may cause him to growl and defend himself. But a dog should not growl at his master; firm treatment will tell him so.

Furniture Sitting

Do you come home and find your dog in your favorite chair? Next thing you know, he will have your slippers and your paper too. This is a habit which should be broken, unless you don't mind cleaning bills.

Opposite page: (*Bottom*) Best of Breed at Putnam Kennel Club in 1982. The mighty "Devil D", more formally Champion Eagle's Devil "D" with his handler Carlos Rojas. This famed record-holding and Best in Show Doberman is owned by Dr. and Mrs. Anthony Di Nardo.

Remove the dog firmly. Perhaps you can provide a comfortable spot in the living room for him so he can be with you. If it continues, some trainers advocate setting a little mousetrap under some paper on the chair. The noise will frighten him off. This can be used; but if you are inclined to worry over noses and toes, try a child's squeaky toy or crackly paper.

Food Stealing

Dogs who steal food are both impolite and dangerous to themselves. If your dog does take food he may be eating the wrong foods and ruining that careful diet you prepared, or perhaps he may eat a poisonous substance. Train him to take food only from his dinner plate, at his dinner hour, or on special occasions when you offer a treat. A loud "No" when your dog reaches for forbidden food and general disapproval may work, but you can also try pepper on the enticing tidbit.

Dogs sometimes have other annoying habits which can be cured using much the same methods described here. Kindness and consistency are important, and reward for good behavior will reinforce your dog's good habits and discourage bad ones.

Special Training for Showing

There are many excellent books describing the type of training you need for showing and obedience trials. Two to be highly recommended are *Successful Dog Show Exhibiting* by Anna Katherine Nicholas and *All About Dog Shows* by Sam Kohl.

The title of Companion Dog (C.D.) in the Novice Class is awarded if your dog can heel on leash, stand for examination by the judge, heel free of the leash, come when called, stay sitting for a time, and lie down for several minutes. When this hurdle is passed, your dog is ready to earn his C.D.X. ("X" for "Excellent"). This requires that he successfully complete more complicated exercises, as well as jump over obstacles and retrieve objects.

He then enters the Utility Class and can compete in tests including scent discrimination, signal exercises, directed jumping, and group exams. The final test is a tracking exercise, and with that he earns his U.D.T. ("T" for "Tracking"), the Ph.D. of the Obedience Class.

Dog Training Classes

Many dogs are sent by their owners to professional trainers. This is essential when there is no one at home to supervise a dog and teach him his *p's* and *q's*. Or perhaps the dog is quite large and active and a trainer is necessary. Another reason might be that you plan to show the dog or place him in obedience trials and you want professional help. If your dog has been badly trained or frightened, you may want such a person to straighten him out. Be prepared for fees which may be high. Your veterinarian or breeder can probably recommend a trainer, or you can look through the many dog publications. Be sure when you take the dog home that you receive full instructions on how to handle him and the proper words to use.

Many communities sponsor classes for dogs. The local S.P.C.A. or humane society may hold inexpensive classes, or the local dog club may sponsor one. The cost of the classes is generally modest. You will long remember attending the first class of the year in your home town. What bedlam, what a commotion! People and dogs will be pulled all over the place. But by the time the class is underway and in the following weeks, calm, more or less, will reign. You can check with friends or with your veterinarian to see if the classes are effective and the teacher qualified. But don't think that all you will have to do is to attend classes and your dog will be the perfect lady or gentleman. You must be prepared to practice what you *both* have learned when you go home. The advantages of a training class for dogs are that you do obtain the services of a professional who can teach you how to do it and that the dog becomes accustomed to other dogs and strangers.

Most dogs prefer people to other dogs; they are truly man's companion. But they must learn to respect other dogs and not fight with them. Fights are dangerous both to dogs and the bystanders. If your dog does get into a dogfight, don't step in unless you are prepared to get bitten or scratched. He may be so excited that your dog may not even know you. Cold water from a hose is often effective. If you have guts, you can wade in and grab the most aggressive dog. Hold him tightly by the collar or the throat until he is half choked. He will generally let go. Neighbors who cooperate and keep their dogs in, or penned in runs, rarely have these problems.

Dobermans and Training

The Doberman has a reputation, in many places, for viciousness. This is untrue. The Doberman has been used extensively in police and army work it is true, but he is perfectly under control then. The Doberman is a one-man dog and generally merely tolerates others around him. He is safe with and protective of children. He makes an excellent watchdog. His training should follow the same general procedures as for other dogs. Because he is a big and strong dog, you may have to jerk his lead a bit harder or pull a little more, but rough treatment will do more harm than good. Never try to train your Doberman in defensive tactics—this should be left to police and army dogs and may cause you grief if used improperly.

To summarize—training is fundamental if you and your Doberman are to live together in harmony. A well-trained dog is both obedient and happy, not cowed or vicious. This can best be accomplished by training him with kindness, firmness, consistency, and the proper rewards for good behavior.

Traveling with Your Dog

When you travel with your dog, to shows or on vacation or wherever, remember that everyone does not share our enthusiasm or love for dogs and that those who do not, strange creatures though they seem to us, have their rights, too. These rights, on which we should not encroach, include not being disturbed, annoyed, or made uncomfortable by the presence and behavior of other people's pets. Your dog should be kept on lead in public places and should recognize and promptly obey the commands "Down," "Come," "Sit," and "Stay."

Take along his crate if you are going any distance with your dog. And keep him in it when riding in the car. A crated dog has a far better chance of escaping injury than one riding loose in the car should an accident occur or an emergency arise. If you do permit your dog to ride loose, never allow him to hang out a window, ears blowing in the breeze. An injury to his eyes could occur in this manner. He could also become overly excited by something he sees and jump out, or he could lose his balance and fall out.

Never, ever, under any circumstances, should a dog be permitted to ride loose in the back of a pick-up truck. It is cruel and shocking that some people do transport dogs in this manner. How easily such a dog can be thrown out of the truck by sudden jolts or an impact! And many dogs have jumped out at the sight of something exciting along the way. Some unthinking individuals tie the dog, probably not realizing that were he to jump under those circumstances, his neck would be broken, he could be dragged alongside the vehicle, or he could be hit by another vehicle. If you are for any reason taking your dog in an open back truck, please have sufficient regard for that dog to at least provide a crate for him, and then remember that, in or out of a crate, a

An early photo of air travel for dogs showing Peggy Adamson (*right*), breeder and shipper of these fine Dobermans. Damasyn The Shawn (*left*) and Damasyn The Aurien (*right*) are on their way to their new owner, Prince Bhanuband Yukol.

dog riding under the direct rays of the sun in hot weather can suffer and have his life endangered by the heat.

If you are staying at a hotel or motel with your dog, exercise him somewhere other than in the flower beds and parking lot of the property. People walking to and from their cars really are not thrilled at "stepping in something" left by your dog. Should an accident occur, pick it up with a tissue or a paper towel and deposit it in a proper receptacle; do not just walk off leaving it to remain there. Usually there are grassy areas on the sides of and behind motels where dogs can be exercised. Use them rather than the more conspicuous, usually carefully tended, front areas or those close to the rooms. If you are becoming a dog show enthusiast, you will eventually need an exercise pen to take with you to the show. Exercise pens are ideal to use when staying at motels, too, as they permit you to limit the dog's roaming space and to pick up after him more easily.

Never leave your dog unattended in the room of a motel unless you are absolutely, positively certain that he will stay there quietly and not damage or destroy anything. You do not want a long list of complaints from irate guests, caused by the annoying barking or whining of a lonesome dog in strange surroundings or an overzealous watch dog barking furiously each time a footstep passes the door or he hears a sound from an adjoining room. And you certainly do not want to return to torn curtains or bedspreads, soiled rugs, or other embarrassing evidence of the fact that your dog is not really house-reliable after all.

If yours is a dog accustomed to traveling with you and you are positive that his behavior will be acceptable when left alone, that is fine. But if the slightest uncertainty exists, the wise course is to leave him in the car while you go to dinner or elsewhere; then bring him into the room when you are ready to retire for the night.

When you travel with a dog, it is often simpler to take along from home the food and water he will need rather than buying food and looking for water while you travel. In this way he will have the rations to which he is accustomed and which you know agree with him, and there will be no fear of problems due to different drinking water. Feeding on the road is quite easy now, at least for short trips, with all the splendid dry prepared foods and high-quality canned meats available. A variety of lightweight, refillable water containers can be bought at many types of stores.

If you are going to another country, you will need a health certificate from your veterinarian for each dog you are taking with you, certifying that each has had rabies shots within the required time preceding your visit.

Be careful always to leave sufficient openings to ventilate your car when the dog will be alone in it. Remember that during the summer, the rays of the sun can make an inferno of a closed car within only a few minutes, so leave enough window space open to provide air circulation. Again, if your dog is in a crate, this can be done quite safely. The fact that you have left the car in a shady spot is not always a guarantee that you will find conditions the same when you return. Don't forget that the position of the sun changes in a matter of minutes, and the car you left nicely shaded half an hour ago can be getting full sunlight far more quickly than you may realize. So, if you leave a dog in the car, make sure there is sufficient ventilation and check back frequently to ascertain that all is well.

134

Chapter 11

Grooming and Exercising Your Doberman

There is nothing more beautiful than a healthy, well-groomed Doberman Pinscher with his shining coat, alert eyes, and athletic stance. As the preceding chapters have told how to make your Doberman healthy and happy, this chapter will show you how to make his appearance reflect the care you have given to your dog.

As owners of dogs, we know that both we and our dogs delight in compliments. By regular grooming and careful provision for exercising, we can doubly reward our pet with well-earned praise and a happy, healthy life.

Training for Pleasurable Grooming

Grooming is a matter of habit for both dog and master. Regular grooming should be a pleasurable occasion for both; it will be, if your pet is accustomed to being combed and brushed. Start the training of your dog early, be kind but firm, and you will find that he will soon begin to enjoy his grooming sessions.

The first thing to teach your Doberman is *patience* during grooming. Don't let him get away with impatient behavior—after all, who's the boss, anyway?

He must learn to stand quietly while being combed and brushed. This is mostly a matter of starting early in his life. Some breeders begin to brush the pups while they are still in the nest, and as a result they have no difficulty when the pups grow up.

Since the best place to groom a dog is on a table or bench, you should train your Doberman Pinscher to jump onto the table or bench, preferably on command. "Table" is the command used by most breeders, and the dog's fondness for grooming will simplify your task.

At the start, or if your pet is nervous (or if you are!), attach his leash to a hook above the table or bench. This will hold him in place. If your dog is very young or nervous, start your grooming activities from the rear, so that he can get accustomed to the new sensations.

Your Doberman's Coat

A dog's coat is a direct reflection of his heredity, diet, and general health, shown to its best by grooming. Proper care of the coat will assure that it is shiny and free from parasites and coat or skin ailments.

The skin and coat of all dogs have certain general characteristics in common. Dogs' skin contain oil glands (which secrete oil to keep the coat shining and waterproof), the sebaceous glands (related to hair growth), and some sweat glands. The sebaceous glands secrete a waxy substance called sebum, which coats the hair as it grows. It is this substance which you may find coating your dog's collar, and it sometimes accounts for that "doggy" odor.

The skin of dogs is much like that of human beings, and do not be surprised if your dog occasionally develops dandruff, since the skin continually sheds and renews itself.

Most breeds of dogs have two coats: a soft undercoat and an outer-coat. The Doberman Pinscher does not have an undercoat (he is allowed, by the A.K.C. standard, to have an invisible gray undercoat on the neck), which accounts for his sleek look. In any event, dogs generally shed at least once a year, and some seem to shed all year round. We know that the increasing length of daylight hours in spring is one factor causing shedding. Dogs who live primarily indoors and are exposed to artificial light may shed more often or even throughout the year.

Combing and Brushing

It is a good idea to groom your Doberman at least once a week or, if you have the time, once a day. This will give your dog a shining look. The Doberman is one of the easiest dogs to keep neat and well groomed, since he is naturally so. Most Dobermans need not be combed before they are brushed, unless they are very dirty. A suitable sturdy comb which will not break or bend can be obtained in any pet store. When combing this short-haired dog, be careful to avoid scraping his skin. If

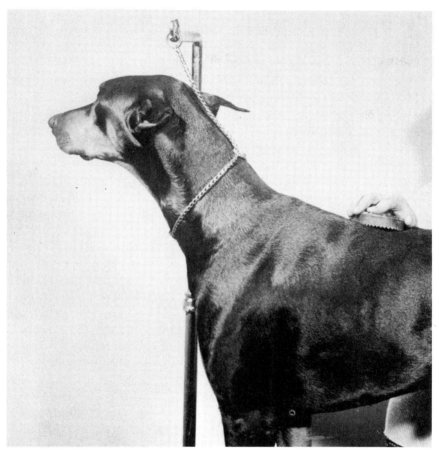
If well groomed, a Doberman's coat will glisten. Brushing removes excess oil that traps dust which causes the coat to appear dull and unattractive.

there are any mats, tease them apart; the use of a little oil will make this task easier. Mats that are cut leave an unsightly bald spot. Burrs should also be removed without the use of scissors.

Brush your Doberman carefully after any necessary combing. While most dogs need very stiff brushes, Dobermans need only a moderately stiff brush. Brush in the direction of the coat until it is smooth and shining. A hound glove may be used to give an extra gleam for special occasions. You will find that your dog gets much pleasure from this phase of grooming. Both comb and brush should be cleaned after each use (the comb is helpful in cleaning the brush) and then stored in the open to air out.

Nail Clipping

Long nails can force a dog's toes outward and permanently affect his stance if they occur during puppyhood. If you enjoy an occasional romp with your pet, you will find it safer for both you and your clothing to keep the nails clipped.

Your veterinarian can clip your dog's nails as part of his regular check-up, or you can do the job with the aid of a pair of special nail clippers for dogs. Do it yourself! The part you must trim is the hook, the section of the nail which curves down. Be careful not to cut into the quick (the vein running through the nail), as it bleeds profusely. In small pups or light-haired dogs, the line where the vein begins is easy to spot. The adult Doberman's nails are dark, but shining a flashlight under the nail can help you to spot the quick.

Are you nervous about clipping? Then file the nails. A good file can do an excellent job of shortening nails, or the file can be used to finish the job after the nails are clipped. Your pet shop supplies these files.

If you do cut into the dog's toes, it is not tragic. Apply styptic powder until the bleeding has stopped.

Most people find that their dog's nails need trimming about every two months. But if your dog walks mostly on concrete sidewalks, his nails will wear down naturally, and he may never need clipping.

Teeth

A little care goes a long way. Tartar is your dog's worst tooth problem. Dog biscuits and bones made from nylon are excellent to keep tartar from forming. The authors do not recommend giving meat bones to dogs, even as "toothbrushes." If heavy tartar does form, it can best be removed by a veterinarian.

Sometimes puppy teeth do not fall out on time and must be pulled to make room for the second teeth. Your veterinarian can check for this when your puppy is in for his regular examination.

If your Doberman has "bad breath," check the condition of his mouth and then his diet.

Ears and Eyes

It is best to leave a dog's ears alone. More damage is done by probing than by disease. If your Doberman's ears appear dirty or full of wax, you can clean them out gently with a cotton-tipped swab. But do not thrust the swab into the ear canal.

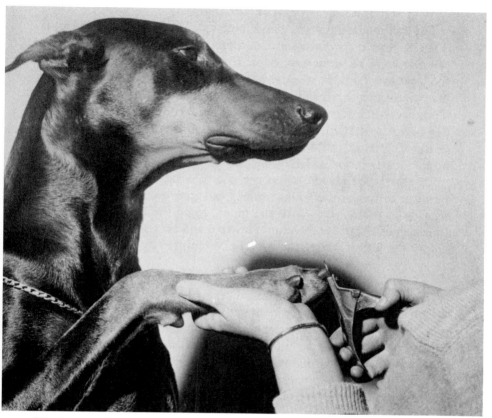

Clipping your Doberman's nails çan be easy and painless, provided you know the right technique and use the correct equipment.

You may at some time see your dog scratching his ears along the ground or shaking his head violently. He may have some sort of irritation such as canker in his ear. Check with your veterinarian. He may recommend that you fill the ear with a preparation such as propylene glycol or mineral oil. To do this, put the dog on a table, hold the ear flap so that you can see the ear canal, and pour the oil into the ear until it is filled. Then massage the base of the ear, wiping up the oil that escapes. This treatment dissolves the wax.

Some dogs have hair growing in the ear canal. This is easily removed by using a tweezer or your fingers to pull it out.

The eyes rarely need grooming care. If they exude a little matter, it is an easy thing to wipe it out with a piece of moist cotton.

Anal Glands

The anal glands are two glands situated on either side of the anus. They appear to serve the same purpose as those of a skunk, and they can also leave an unpleasant odor. If a dog is extremely frightened or the loser in a fight, he releases the contents of the glands. The glands may become enlarged and infected if they are not naturally discharged. To prevent infection, they must be emptied from time to time. If your dog begins to drag himself around on his tail and there is a swollen appearance around the anus, check the glands. If you feel two hard lumps, it's time for action.

To empty the glands, stand the dog in a tub or use a big wad of tissue or cotton, as the liquid you will extract is quite smelly. With one hand hold the tail up. With the other, using the thumb and middle finger, gently squeeze each lump upward and outward. If this does not empty the glands, they may have to be emptied by a veterinarian.

Bathing

It seems incredible that nearly every puppy owner believes it is wrong to bathe a puppy, or let it get wet, until the pup is six months old. No one likes to advise on such a point because of the usual unscientific method of thinking which causes too many people to feel that because one event follows another, the first is the cause of the second. If you advise a client to bathe her dog and a week later the pup has pneumonia, you are to blame—you and the bath. Therefore we do not advise you. We can say we've never known of a bath in a warm house, after which the pup was dried, to produce pneumonia, and we have known of hundreds of cases of pneumonia in puppies which had not had baths or been exposed or wet. On the basis of our experience, it is much more likely that a puppy will develop pneumonia if he is not given a bath.

But, to be sensible, we all know that every puppy was born soaking wet and dried from his own body heat and that of his mother's. If one of your puppies gets dirty or smelly, bathe him, not before.

Today there are many ways of bathing puppies. Use special dog soap, cake or liquid. Do not use baby soaps or household soaps, cake or liquid. You can give him a "dry bath" by using a special dog preparation made in any of several ways. These are usually special detergents in which bug-killing preparations are incorporated. Some leave an insecticidal residue; some do not. Some are of a dry, cornmeal powder base, some of foaming whipped-cream consistency.

140

Ch. Bailes Apache of Gracewood with handler Ed Bracey (*left*) and judge Robert A. Moseley (*right*). Owned and bred by Mrs. Boyce Bailes.

Bathing is accomplished by selecting a proper place to start with. The size and condition of the puppy help to determine the place. A month-old toy puppy may be washed in a pot, while a six-month-old large size dog needs nothing smaller than the family bathtub. If you don't mind using the tub after the dog, you can use your own. Thousands of dog owners do. Or, if you wish, you can rig up a special tub for your pet.

The first thing to do if you are giving a water bath is to get the soap mixture ready. Have another pan with warm water in which is mixed some dog parasite preparation, of which several are available. Put a cotton plug in each ear of the pup and he will be less inclined to shake himself. Also put on an apron of some waterproof material to protect yourself in the event the pup struggles or shakes.

Ch. Damasyn The Tassi, C.D., by Ch. Dictator von Glenhugel ex Isolde von Gruenewald, bred by Mrs. Bob Adamson and owned by Carl Hester.

The experienced dog washer realizes that water runs off his dog's back and only slowly wets the hair and penetrates to the skin. Soap is a wetting agent. Therefore he soaps the dog as he wets him. Work up a lather by rubbing and rinse the dog thoroughly, making sure that all the soap is washed out of the coat. If there is still dirt to be seen or the odor is not gone, soap and rinse again.

When bathing your dog, squeeze all the water you can from the dog's coat and apply the rinse. This kills any passengers and leaves a clean, fresh odor. Now rub the dog as dry as you can with a towel and leave him where he will finish drying in a warm place.

If you prefer to give him a dry bath, follow the directions on the container of whatever you buy. If a coarse powder is used, be sure to comb and brush your dog thoroughly before you allow him his freedom. This method can clean a dog well. If you use a foaming detergent, rub it in and wipe it off thoroughly with a towel. Applying the detergent and dissolving the dirt without removing it does no good, except to kill insects. The dirt is still on the coat; and when the pup is given his freedom, he either wipes the dirt off on the rugs, furniture, or your clothes, or else it dries on him and the "bath" proves to be no bath at all.

The matter of drying is really important, especially in cold weather. Many puppy owners wash their charges in the evening, and the pups have to stay inside where it is warm to finish drying.

As puppies grow older, body odors become more pronounced. Ear canker may develop and perfume the air in the puppy's proximity

Ch. Damasyn The Sonnet, by Ch. Dictator von Glenhugel ex Damasyn The Song, bred by Peggy Adamson, and owned by Peggy Adamson and Agnes Johnson Eathorne.

with the odor of bad cheese. The pup's anal glands may become infected and he may slide along your rugs, leaving an obnoxious odor. His collar or harness may accumulate the waxy secretion from his skin and acquire the typical doggy odor.

You can bathe your pup often, but such odors remain to taunt you. However, if you treat the ear canker with what your veterinarian gives you, empty the pup's anal glands occasionally, and scrape the collar, cleansing it with alcohol and then oiling it, the pup will smell sweet and clean after a bath.

Whatever you do, *don't use human products on dogs.* Soaps and shampoos made for humans are too alkaline for dogs' coats and can actually ruin them.

Special Problems

Parasites

Lice and fleas are discussed in the chapter on diseases, but oftentimes routine control of these annoying pests can be part of grooming. If you suspect one of these problems, you can bathe your pet with any of the preparations on the market for flea control. Once you spot fleas, be sure to give the kennel and bedding a good bath too. Many professional kennel owners deflea their dogs' quarters regularly. If you keep both dog and bed free from these pests, chances are he won't suffer from them.

Skunks

If your dog tangles with a skunk, the skunk will probably be the winner. Unfortunately, both you and the dog are losers. Don't take off in the other direction when he comes home after one of these encounters. Wash him thoroughly and put him near the heat or out in the sun. The odor will disappear in time. Some people advocate washing the animal in tomato juice, but we have not tried this technique as yet.

Paint

The best chemical with which to remove paint is kerosene. Rub off the paint as soon as possible with a cloth dipped in kerosene, and then wash it off well. Kerosene can burn an animal's skin, so apply it with care.

Keep your Doberman from chewing on paint which is on his fur, as it may contain poisonous substances.

144

Tar

If the roads in your neighborhood have been recently tarred, rest assured that your dog will have investigated. He may then come home with tar on his feet or coat. To remove tar, wipe off the tar with kerosene, as noted above; don't forget to wash off the kerosene residue. It may take several treatments. Fortunately, the Doberman's sleek, short coat minimizes paint and tar problems.

Exercise

Exercise is "doing what comes naturally" for most Dobermans. If left completely free, your dog could be found running over the fields and woods. But crowded urban areas and their special requirements of breeding and control impose restrictions on a dog's exercising.

The Doberman in the city should be exercised regularly by walking, which he will greatly enjoy. Most cities and towns require that dogs be on a leash when out in the street, but this should not prevent your dog from getting the full benefit from the walk. He will get the rest of his exercise in the house or apartment playing with you or the children of the household or with his toys.

Even dogs as large as the Doberman Pinscher can get enough exercise in what seems to be a limited space. In a kennel, a run of 10 X 25 feet is adequate.

The authors believe that a run is better than complete freedom. A run does not rule out walks or an occasional session in the woods and fields. One of the larger dogs in our neighborhood spends the winter towing kids on an old-fashioned sled. Many dogs enjoy swimming and gleefully jump into the water in pursuit of a ball or stick or simply to chase a friend.

If you give your dog adequate exercise and proper grooming, diet, and medical care, he will reward you with compliments from the neighbors and perhaps even a blue ribbon at the dog show!

Ch. Wynterwynd's Me 'N My Shadow, by Ch. Elexa's Final Flair of Selena ex Wynterwynd's Rusty Nail, winning a four-point "major" under judge Robert S. Forsyth at the Doberman Pinscher Club of Dallas Specialty in 1983, handled by Kathleen Pollack. Phil and Jill Leath, owners, Albuquerque, New Mexico.

Chapter 12

The Making of a Show Dog

If you have decided to become a show dog exhibitor, you have accepted a very real and very exciting challenge. The groundwork has been accomplished with the selection of your future show prospect. If you have purchased a puppy, we assume that you have gone through all the proper preliminaries concerning good care, which should be the same if the puppy is a pet or future show dog with a few added precautions for the latter.

General Considerations

Remember the importance of keeping your future winner in trim, top condition. Since you want him neither too fat nor too thin, his appetite for his proper diet should be guarded, and children and guests should not be permitted to constantly be feeding him "goodies." The best treat of all is a small wad of raw ground beef or a packaged dog treat. To be avoided are ice cream, cake, cookies, potato chips, and other fattening items which will cause the dog to put on weight and may additionally spoil his appetite for the proper, nourishing, well-balanced diet so essential to good health and condition.

The importance of temperament and showmanship cannot possibly be overestimated. They have put many a mediocre dog across while lack of them can ruin the career of an otherwise outstanding specimen. From the day your dog joins your family, socialize him. Keep him accustomed to being with people and to being handled by people. Encourage your friends and relatives to "go over" him as the judges will in the ring so this will not seem a strange and upsetting experience. Practice showing his "bite" (the manner in which his teeth meet) quickly and deftly. It is quite simple to slip the lips apart with your fingers, and the puppy should be willing to accept this from you or the judge without struggle. This is also true of further mouth examination when necessary. Where the standard demands examination of the roof of the mouth and the tongue, accustom the dog to having his jaws opened wide in order for the judge to make this required examination. When missing teeth must be noted, again, teach the dog to permit his jaws to be opened wide and his side lips separated as judges will need to check them one or both of these ways.

Some judges prefer that the exhibitors display the dog's bite and other mouth features themselves. These are the considerate ones, who do not wish to chance the spreading of possible infection from dog to dog with their hands on each one's mouth—a courtesy particularly appreciated in these days of virus epidemics. But the old-fashioned judges still persist in doing it themselves, so the dog should be ready for either possibility.

Take your future show dog with you in the car, thus accustoming him to riding so that he will not become carsick on the day of a dog show. He should associate pleasure and attention with going in the car, or van or motor home. Take him where it is crowded: downtown, to the shops, everywhere you go that dogs are permitted. Make the expeditions fun for him by frequent petting and words of praise; do not just ignore him as you go about your errands.

Do not overly shelter your future show dog. Instinctively you may want to keep him at home where he is safe from germs or danger. This can be foolish on two counts. The first reason is that a puppy kept away from other dogs builds up no natural immunity against all the things with which he will come in contact at dog shows, so it is wiser actually to keep him well up to date on all protective shots and then let him become accustomed to being among dogs and dog owners. Also, a dog who never is among strange people, in strange places, or among strange dogs, may grow up with a shyness or timidity of spirit that will cause you real problems as his show career draws near.

Keep your show prospect's coat in immaculate condition with frequent grooming and daily brushing. When bathing is necessary, use a shampoo made especially for dogs and available at pet shops or use whatever the breeder of your puppy may suggest. Several of the brand-name products do an excellent job. Be sure to rinse thoroughly so as not to risk skin irritation by traces of soap left behind and protect against soap entering the eyes by a drop of castor oil in each before you lather up. Use warm water (be sure it is not uncomfortably hot or chillingly cold) and a good spray. A hair dryer is a real convenience and can be used for thorough drying after first blotting off the excess moisture with a turkish towel. A wad of cotton in each ear will prevent water entering the ear cavity.

Formation of mats should be watched for carefully, especially behind the ears and underneath the armpits. Toenails also should be watched and trimmed whenever necessary. It is important not to permit nails to grow excessively long, as they will ruin the appearance of both the feet and pasterns.

Assuming that you will be handling the dog yourself, or even if he will be professionally handled, a few moments each day of dog show routine is important. Practice setting him up as you have seen the exhibitors do at the shows you've attended, and teach him to hold this position once you have him stacked to your satisfaction. Make the learning period pleasant by being firm but lavish in your praise when he responds correctly. Teach him to gait at your side at a moderate rate on a loose lead. When you have mastered the basic essentials at home, then hunt out and join a training class for future work. Training classes are sponsored by show-giving clubs in many areas, and their popularity is steadily increasing. If you have no other way of locating one, perhaps your veterinarian would know of one through some of his other clients; but if you are sufficiently aware of the dog show world to want a show dog, you will probably be personally acquainted with other people who will share information of this type with you.

Accustom your show dog to being in a crate (which you should be doing with a pet dog as well). He should relax in his crate at the shows "between times" for his own well being and safety.

A show dog's teeth must be kept clean and free of tartar. Hard dogbiscuits can help toward this, but if tartar accumulates, see that it is removed promptly by your veterinarian. Bones are not suitable for show dogs as they tend to damage and wear down the tooth enamel.

Match Shows

Your show dog's initial experience in the ring should be in match show competition for several reasons. First, this type of event is intended as a learning experience for both the dog and the exhibitor. You will not feel embarrassed or out of place no matter how poorly your puppy may behave or how inept your attempts at handling may be, as you will find others there with the same type of problems. The

Tasha of Talacon winning her title at Troy K.C. 1975.

Opposite page: Ch. Sherluck's Barney Miller, by Ch. Sherluck's L.B. Jake ex Ch. Morago Hills High Fashion Wac. Bred and handled by Faye Strauss of Kent, Washington, she is owned by Esther and Robert Holmes of Bellevue, Washington. Pictured winning points towards her title at Greater Clark County in 1983.

Practice stacking your Doberman at home so he will become accustomed to the procedure for a perfect show stance.

important thing is that you get the puppy out and into a show ring where the two of you can practice together and learn the ropes.

Only on rare occasions is it necessary to make match show entries in advance, and even those with a pre-entry policy will usually accept entries at the door as well. Thus you need not plan several weeks ahead, as is the case with point shows, but can go when the mood strikes you. Also there is a vast difference in the cost, as match show entries only cost a few dollars while entry fees for the point shows may be over ten dollars, an amount none of us needs to waste until we have some idea of how the puppy will behave or how much more pre-show training is needed.

Match shows very frequently are judged by professional handlers who, in addition to making the awards, are happy to help new exhibitors with comments and advice on their puppies and their presentation of them. Avail yourself of all these opportunities before heading out to the sophisticated world of the point shows.

Ch. Eagle's Devil "D" with his handler, Carlos Rojas. This memorable Doberman, winner of the 1984 Doberman Pinscher Club of America National Specialty, and Number 1 Doberman Pinscher for that year, the latter for the third consecutive year, has won first in more than 70 Working Groups, has 18 Bests in Show, and close to two hundred Bests of Breed, including 10 Specialty Shows. A homebred belonging to Dr. and Mrs. Anthony Di Nardo, East Hartford, Connecticut.

Australian Ch. Stehle Binda, bred, owned and exhibited by D. Eschbach, Stehle Kennels, is a multi Best in Show and in Group winner. She was Challenge Certificate winning bitch and Best of Breed at the 1983 Spring Fair Dog Show judged by Robert S. Forsyth of the United States.

Ch. Pajant's Encore v Rockelle, Number 2 Doberman in the United States for 1982, during 1983 won 50 Bests of Breed, 11 Groups, 22 Group placements, an all-breed Best in Show, and several Specialties. A Doberman Pinscher Top Twenty dog, already a successful sire with many noted bitches bred to him. Dot Roberts, owner, New City, N.Y. "Cory" pictured, handled by Terry Lazzaro Hundt winning the Working Group at Eastern Dog Club, 1983, Robert Forsyth judging.

Point Shows

As previously mentioned, entries for American Kennel Club point shows must be made in advance. This must be done on an official entry blank of the show-giving club. The entry must then be filed either personally or by mail with the show superintendent or the show secretary (if the event is being run by the club members alone and a superintendent has not been hired, this information will appear on the premium list) in time to reach its destination prior to the published closing date or filling of the quota. These entries must be made carefully, must be signed by the owner of the dog or the owner's agent (your professional handler), and must be accompanied by the entry fee; otherwise they will not be accepted. Remember that it is not when the entry leaves your hands that counts but the date of arrival at its destination. If you are relying on the mails, which are not always dependable, get the entry off well before the deadline to avoid disappointment.

A dog must be entered at a dog show in the name of the actual owner at the time of the entry closing date of that specific show. If a registered dog has been acquired by a new owner, it must be entered in the name of the new owner in any show for which entries close after the date of acquirement, regardless of whether the new owner has or has not actually received the registration certificate indicating that the dog is recorded in his name. State on the entry form whether or not transfer application has been mailed to the American Kennel Club, and it goes without saying that the latter should be attended to promptly when you purchase a registered dog.

In filling out your entry blank, type, print, or write clearly, paying particular attention to the spelling of names, correct registration numbers, and so on. Also, if there is more than one variety in your breed, be sure to indicate into which category your dog is being entered.

The Puppy Class is for dogs or bitches who are six months of age and under twelve months, were whelped in the United States, and are not champions. The age of a dog shall be calculated up to and inclusive of the first day of a show. For example, the first day a dog whelped on January 1st is eligible to compete in a Puppy Class at a show is July 1st of the same year; and he may continue to compete in Puppy Classes up to and including a show on December 31st of the same year, but he is *not* eligible to compete in a Puppy Class at a show held on or after January 1st of the following year.

The Puppy Class is the first one in which you should enter your puppy. In it a certain allowance will be made for the fact that they *are*

155

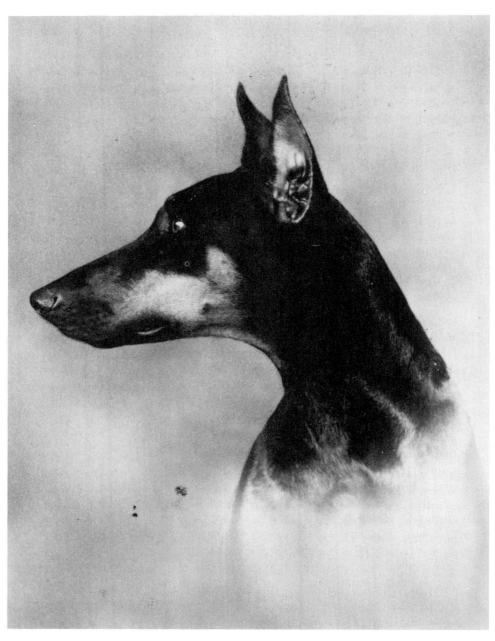

This distinguished Doberman is Shady Acres Endless Summer, C.D., SchH III, VB, WH, AD. by Sandy's Derringer Dirk, U.D.T., SchH. II ex Shady Acres Foxfire, C.D. Bred by Nanci Little. Owned by Anita Chandler, Miami, Florida.

puppies, thus an immature dog or one displaying less than perfect showmanship will be less severely penalized than, for instance, would be the case in Open. It is also quite likely that others in the class will be suffering from these problems, too. When you enter a puppy, be sure to check the classification with care, as some shows divide their Puppy Class into a 6-9 months old section and a 9-12 months old section.

The Novice Class is for dogs six months of age and over, whelped in the United States or Canada, who *prior to the official closing date for entries* have *not* won three first prizes in the Novice Class, any first prize at all in the Bred-by-Exhibitor, American-bred, or Open Classes, or one or more points toward championship. The provisions for this class are confusing to many people, which is probably the reason exhibitors do not enter in it more frequently. A dog may win any number of first prizes in the Puppy Class and still retain his eligibility for Novice. He may place second, third or fourth not only in Novice on an unlimited number of occasions but also in Bred-by-Exhibitor, American-bred and Open and still remain eligible for Novice. But he may no longer be shown in Novice when he has won three blue ribbons in that class, when he has won even one blue ribbon in either Bred-by-Exhibitor, American-bred, or Open, or when he has won a single championship point.

In determining whether or not a dog is eligible for the Novice Class, keep in mind the fact that previous wins are calculated according to the official published date for closing of entries, not by the date on which you may actually have made the entry. So if in the interim, between the time you made the entry and the official closing date, your dog makes a win causing him to become ineligible for Novice, change your class *immediately* to another for which he will be eligible, preferably such as either Bred-by-Exhibitor or American-bred. To do this, you must contact the show's superintendent or secretary, at first by telephone to save time and at the same time confirm it in writing. The Novice Class always seems to have the fewest entries of any class, and therefore it is a splendid "practice ground" for you and your young dog while you are getting the "feel" of being in the ring.

Bred-by-Exhibitor Class is for dogs whelped in the United States or, if individually registered in the American Kennel Club Stud Book, for dogs whelped in Canada who are six months of age or older, are not champions, and are owned wholly or in part by the person or by the spouse of the person who was the breeder or one of the breeders of record. Dogs entered in this class must be handled in the class by an owner or by a member of the immediate family of the owner.

Members of an immediate family for this purpose are husband, wife, father, mother, son, daughter, brother, or sister. This is the class which is really the "breeders' showcase," and the one which breeders should enter with particular pride to show off their achievements.

The American-bred Class is for all dogs excepting champions, six months of age or older, who were whelped in the United States by reason of a mating which took place in the United States.

The Open Class is for any dog six months of age or older (this is the only restriction for this class). Dogs with championship points compete in it, dogs who are already champions are eligible to do so, dogs who are imported can be entered, and, of course, American-bred dogs compete in it. This class is, for some strange reason, the favorite of exhibitors who are "out to win." They rush to enter their pointed dogs in it, under the false impression that by doing so they assure themselves of greater attention from the judges. This really is not so, and to enter in one of the less competitive classes, with a better chance of winning it and thus earning a second opportunity of gaining the judge's approval by returning to the ring in the Winners Class, can often be a more effective strategy.

One does not enter for the Winners Class. One earns the right to compete in it by winning first prize in Puppy, Novice, Bred-by-Exhibitor, American-bred, or Open. No dog who has been defeated on the same day in one of these classes is eligible to compete for Winners, and every dog who has been a blue-ribbon winner in one of them and not defeated in another, should he have been entered in more than one class, (as occasionally happens) *must* do so. Following the selection of the Winners Dog or the Winners Bitch, the dog or bitch receiving that award leaves the ring. Then the dog or bitch who placed second in that class, unless previously beaten by another dog or bitch in another class at the same show, re-enters the ring to compete against the remaining first-prize winners for Reserve. The latter award indicates that the dog or bitch selected for it is standing "in reserve" should the one who received Winners be disqualified or declared ineligible through any technicality when the awards are checked at the American Kennel Club. In that case, the one who placed Reserve is moved up to Winners, at the same time receiving the appropriate championship points.

Winners Dog and Winners Bitch are the awards which carry points toward championship with them. The points are based on the number of dogs or bitches actually in competition, and the points are scaled one through five, the latter being the greatest number available to any

Ebonaire's Thistledown, by Carosel's B-on-the-Move from Ch. Ebonaire's Chaldea, whose show career was cut short owing to illness in her owner's family. One of the outstanding Dobermans owned by Judy Weiss, Ebonaire Kennels, N.Y.

Uhlan du Fief de la Garenne, handsome young son of Grand Champion Danico Stamm Juon at ten months. Owned by Mr. and Mrs. Mulero, famous Doberman breeders in France.

one dog or bitch at any one show. Three-, four-, or five-point wins are considered majors. In order to become a champion, a dog or bitch must have won two majors under two different judges, plus at least one point from a third judge, and the additional points necessary to bring the total to fifteen. When your dog has gained fifteen points as described above, a championship certificate will be issued to you, and your dog's name will be published in the champions of record list in the *Pure-Bred Dogs/American Kennel Gazette,* the official publication of the American Kennel Club.

The scale of championship points for each breed is worked out by the American Kennel Club and reviewed annually, at which time the number required in competition may be either changed (raised or lowered) or remain the same. The scale of championship points for all breeds is published annually in the May issue of the *Gazette,* and the current ratings for each breed within that area are published in every show catalog.

When a dog or bitch is adjudged Best of Winners, its championship points are, for that show, compiled on the basis of which sex had the greater number of points. If there are two points in dogs and four in bitches and the dog goes Best of Winners, then *both* the dog and the bitch are awarded an equal number of points, in this case four. Should the Winners Dog or the Winners Bitch go on to win Best of Breed or Best of Variety, additional points are accorded for the additional dogs and bitches defeated by so doing, provided, of course, that there were entries specifically for Best of Breed Competition or Specials, as these specific entries are generally called.

If your dog or bitch takes Best of Opposite Sex after going Winners, points are credited according to the number of the same sex defeated in both the regular classes and Specials competition. If Best of Winners is also won, then whatever additional points for each of these awards are available will be credited. Many a one- or two-point win has grown into a major in this manner.

Moving further along, should your dog win its Variety Group from the classes (in other words, if it has taken either Winners Dog or Winners Bitch), you then receive points based on the greatest number of points awarded to any member of any breed included within that Group during that show's competition. Should the day's winning also include Best in Show, the same rule of thumb applies, and your dog or bitch receives the highest number of points awarded to any other dog of any breed at that event.

Ch. Baptiste's War News winning Best in Show with her handler J. Nate Levine. Owned by Mrs. Albert C. Langshaw and bred by Jean L. Baptiste, War News was sired by Ch. Favoriet v Franzhof ex Ch. Fidelia v Tauzieher.

Best of Breed competition consists of the Winners Dog and the Winners Bitch, who automatically compete on the strength of those awards, in addition to whatever dogs and bitches have been entered specifically for this class for which champions of record are eligible. Since July 1980, dogs who, according to their owner's records, have completed the requirements for a championship after the closing of entries for the show, but whose championships are unconfirmed, may be transferred from one of the regular classes to the Best of Breed competition, provided this transfer is made by the show superintendent or show secretary *prior to the start of any judging at the show.*

This has proved an extremely popular new rule, as under it a dog can finish on Saturday and then be transferred and compete as a Special on Sunday. It must be emphasized that the change *must* be made *prior* to the start of *any* part of the day's judging, not for just your individual breed.

161

In the United States, Best of Breed winners are entitled to compete in the Variety Group which includes them. This is not mandatory, it is a privilege which exhibitors value. (In Canada, Best of Breed winners *must* compete in the Variety Group, or they lose any points already won.) The dogs winning *first* in each of the seven Variety Groups *must* compete for Best in Show. Missing the opportunity of taking your dog in for competition in its Group is foolish as it is there where the general public is most likely to notice your breed and become interested in learning about it.

Non-regular classes are sometimes included at the all-breed shows, and they are almost invariably included at Specialty Shows. These include Stud Dog Class and Brood Bitch Class, which are judged on the basis of the quality of the two offspring accompanying the sire or dam. The quality of the latter two is beside the point and should not be considered by the judge; it is the youngsters who count, and the quality of *both* are to be averaged to decide which sire or dam is the best and most consistent producer. Then there is the Brace Class (which, at all-breed shows, moves up to Best Brace in each Variety Group and then Best Brace in Show), which is judged on the similarity and evenness of appearance of the two members of the brace. In other words, the two dogs should look like identical twins in size, color, and conformation and should move together almost as a single dog, one person handling with precision and ease. The same applies to the Team Class competition, except that four dogs are involved and, if necessary, two handlers.

The Veterans Class is for the older dogs, the minimum age of whom is seven years. This class is judged on the quality of the dogs, as the winner competes in Best of Breed competition and has, on a respectable number of occasions, been known to take that top award. So the point is *not* to pick out the oldest dog, as some judges seem to believe, but the best specimen of the breed, exactly as in the regular classes.

Then there are Sweepstakes and Futurity Stakes sponsored by many Specialty clubs, sometimes as part of their regular Specialty Shows and sometimes as separate events on an entirely different occasion. The difference between the two stakes is that Sweepstakes entries usually include dogs from six to eighteen months age with entries made at the same time as the others for the show, while for a Futurity the entries are bitches nominated when bred and the individual puppies entered at or shortly following their birth.

If you already show your dog, if you plan on being an exhibitor in the future, or if you simply enjoy attending dog shows, there is a book, written by Anna Katherine Nicholas, which you will find to be an invaluable source of detailed information about all aspects of show dog competition. This book is *Successful Dog Show Exhibiting* (T.F.H. Publications, Inc.) and is available wherever the one you are reading was purchased.

Junior Showmanship Competition

If there is a youngster in your family between the ages of ten and sixteen, there is no better or more rewarding hobby than becoming an active participant in Junior Showmanship. This is a marvelous activity for young people. It teaches responsibility, good sportsmanship, the fun of competition where one's own skills are the deciding factor of success, proper care of a pet, and how to socialize with other young folks. Any youngster may experience the thrill of emerging from the ring a winner and the satisfaction of a good job well done.

Entry in Junior Showmanship Classes is open to any boy or girl who is at least ten years old and under seventeen years old on the day of the show. The Novice Junior Showmanship Class is open to youngsters who have not already won, at the time the entries close, three firsts in this class. Youngsters who have won three firsts in Novice may compete in the Open Junior Showmanship Class. Any junior handler who wins his third first-place award in Novice may participate in the Open Class at the same show, provided that the Open Class has at least one other junior handler entered and competing in it that day. The Novice and Open Classes may be divided into Junior and Senior Classes. Youngsters between the ages of ten and twelve, inclusively, are eligible for the Junior division; and youngsters between thirteen and seventeen, inclusively, are eligible for the Senior division.

Any of the foregoing classes may be separated into individual classes for boys and for girls. If such a division is made, it must be so indicated on the premium list. The premium list also indicates the prize for Best Junior Handler, if such a prize is being offered at the show. Any youngster who wins a first in any of the regular classes may enter the competition for this prize, provided the youngster has been undefeated in any other Junior Showmanship Class at that show.

Junior Showmanship Classes, unlike regular conformation classes in which the quality of the dog is judged, are judged solely on the skill and ability of the junior handling the dog. Which dog is best is not the point—it is which youngster does the best job with the dog that is under consideration. Eligibility requirements for the dog being shown

163

Ebonaire's Mister Esquire winning the breed at Newtown Kennel Club in August 1964. Handled by J. Monroe Stebbins, Mister Esquire was from the Ebonaire Kennels of Edward and Judy Weiss who have produced so many Dobermans of importance over the years.

in Junior Showmanship, and other detailed information, can be found in *Regulations for Junior Showmanship*, available from the American Kennel Club.

A junior who has a dog that he or she can enter in both Junior Showmanship and conformation classes has twice the opportunity for success and twice the opportunity to get into the ring and work with the dog, a combination which can lead to not only awards for expert handling but also, if the dog is of sufficient quality, for making a conformation champion.

Pre-Show Preparations for Your Dog and You

Preparation of the items you will need as a dog show exhibitor should not be left until the last moment. They should be planned and arranged for at least several days in advance of the show in order for you to remain calm and relaxed as the countdown starts.

The importance of the crate has already been mentioned, and we hope it is already part of your equipment. Of equal importance is the grooming table, which very likely you have also already acquired for use at home. You should take it along with you to the shows, as your dog will need last minute touches before entering the ring. Should you have not yet made this purchase, folding tables with rubber tops are made specifically for this purpose and can be purchased at most dog shows, where concession booths with marvelous assortments of "doggy" necessities are to be found, or at your pet supplier. You will also need a sturdy tack box (also available at the dog show concessions) in which to carry your grooming tools and equipment. The latter should include brushes, comb, scissors, nail clippers, whatever you use for last minute clean-up jobs, cotton swabs, first-aid equipment, and anything you are in the habit of using on the dog, including a leash or two of the type you prefer, some well-cooked and dried-out liver or any of the small packaged "dog treats" for use as bait in the ring, an atomizer in case you wish to dampen your dog's coat when you are preparing him for the ring, and so on. A large turkish towel to spread under the dog on the grooming table is also useful.

Take a large thermos or cooler of ice, the biggest one you can accommodate in your vehicle, for use by "man and beast." Take a jug of water (there are lightweight, inexpensive ones available at all sporting goods shops) and a water dish. If you plan to feed the dog at the show, or if you and the dog will be away from home more than one day, bring food for him from home so that he will have the type to which he is accustomed.

You may or may not have an exercise pen. Many people think that such a pen is a *must*, even if you only have one dog. While the shows do provide areas for the exercise of the dogs, these are among the most likely places to have your dog come in contact with any illnesses which may be going around, and having a pen of your own for your dog's use is excellent protection. Such a pen can be used in other ways, too, such as a place other than the crate in which to put the dog to relax (that is roomier than the crate) and a place in which the dog can exercise at motels and rest areas. These, too, are available at the show concession stands and come in a variety of heights and sizes. A set of "pooper scoopers" should also be part of your equipment, along with a package of plastic bags for cleaning up after your dog.

Bring along folding chairs for the members of your party, unless all of you are fond of standing, as these are almost never provided anymore by the clubs. Have your name stamped on the chairs so that there will be no doubt as to whom the chairs belong. Bring whatever you and your family enjoy for drinks or snacks in a picnic basket or cooler, as show food, in general, is expensive and usually not great. You should always have a pair of boots, a raincoat, and a rain hat with you (they should remain permanently in your vehicle if you plan to attend shows regularly), as well as a sweater, a warm coat, and a change of shoes. A smock or big cover-up apron will assure that you remain tidy as you prepare the dog for the ring. Your overnight case should include a small sewing kit for emergency repairs, bandaids, headache and indigestion remedies, and any personal products or medications you normally use.

In your car you should always carry maps of the area where you are headed and an assortment of motel directories. Generally speaking, we have found Holiday Inns to be the nicest about taking dogs. Ramadas and Howard Johnsons generally do so cheerfully (with a few exceptions). Best Western generally frowns on pets (not always, but often enough to make it necessary to find out which do). Some of the smaller chains welcome pets. The majority of privately owned motels do not.

Have everything prepared the night before the show to expedite your departure. Be sure that the dog's identification and your judging program and other show information are in your purse or briefcase. If you are taking sandwiches, have them ready. Anything that goes into the car the night before the show will be one thing less to remember in the morning. Decide upon what you will wear and have it out and ready. If there is any question in your mind about what to wear, try on the possibilities before the day of the show; don't risk feeling you may want to change when you see yourself dressed a few moments prior to departure time!

In planning your outfit, make it something simple that will not detract from your dog. Remember that a dark dog silhouettes attractively against a light background and vice-versa. Sport clothes always seem to look best at dog shows, preferably conservative in type and not overly "loud" as you do not want to detract from your dog, who should be the focus of interest at this point. What you wear on your

166

D.P.B.A.
PENN-JERSEY
SEPTEMBER 4 1976
SWEEPSTAKES
FIRST PLACE
PUPPY BITCH
9 TO 12 MONTHS
A BUSHMAN PHOTO

Witching Hour's Fraulein, owner handled by Kay Martin, Brooklyn, N.Y.

Ch. D'Mascus Sambuca v Alisaton, C.D. This is the famous "Miss Samsam" who finished her championship at one week over a year's age, along the way beating 138 Dobes on one occasion to win a Specialty Best in Show at only seven months thus taking her first five points. She won the Doberman Pinscher Club of America 1982 award for the most blue ribbons won by a puppy bitch, and is one of three champions in her litter. Co-breeders, Peggy Esposito and Gwen De Milta. Owners, Charles Guardascione and Mary Manning.

A four-month-old Doberman Pinscher already being stacked in preparation for a possible show career.

feet is important. Many types of flooring can be hazardously slippery, as can wet grass. Make it a habit to wear rubber soles and low or flat heels in the ring for your own safety, especially if you are showing a dog that likes to move out smartly.

Your final step in pre-show preparation is to leave yourself plenty of time to reach the show that morning. Traffic can get amazingly heavy as one nears the immediate area of the show, finding a parking place can be difficult, and other delays may occur. You'll be in better humor to enjoy the day if your trip to the show is not fraught with panic over fear of not arriving in time!

169

Enjoying the Dog Show

From the moment of your arrival at the show until after your dog has been judged, keep foremost in your mind the fact that he is your reason for being there and that he should therefore be the center of your attention. Arrive early enough to have time for those last-minute touches that can make such a great difference when he enters the ring. Be sure that he has ample time to exercise and that he attends to personal matters. A dog arriving in the ring and immediately using it as an exercise pen hardly makes a favorable impression on the judge.

When you reach ringside, ask the steward for your arm-card and anchor it firmly into place on your arm. Make sure that you are where you should be when your class is called. The fact that you have picked up your arm-card does not guarantee, as some seem to think, that the judge will wait for you. The judge has a full schedule which he wishes to complete on time. Even though you may be nervous, assume an air of calm self-confidence. Remember that this is a hobby to be enjoyed, so approach it in that state of mind. The dog will do better, too, as he will be quick to reflect your attitude.

Always show your dog with an air of pride. If you make mistakes in presenting him, don't worry about it. Next time you will do better. Do not permit the presence of more experienced exhibitors to intimidate you. After all, they, too, once were newcomers.

The judging routine usually starts when the judge asks that the dogs be gaited in a circle around the ring. During this period the judge is watching each dog as it moves, noting style, topline, reach and drive, head and tail carriage, and general balance. Keep your mind and your eye on your dog, moving him at his most becoming gait and keeping your place in line without coming too close to the exhibitor ahead of you. Always keep your dog on the inside of the circle, between yourself and the judge, so that the judge's view of the dog is unobstructed.

Calmly pose the dog when requested to set up for examination whether on the ground or on a table. If you are at the head of the line and many dogs are in the class, go all the way to the end of the ring before starting to stack the dog, leaving sufficient space for those behind you to line theirs up as well as requested by the judge. If you are not at the head of the line but between other exhibitors, leave sufficient space ahead of your dog for the judge to examine him. The dogs should be spaced so that the judge is able to move among them to see them from all angles. In practicing to "set up" or "stack" your dog for the judge's examination, bear in mind the importance of doing so

Hoss von Klosterholz on the way to the title. Saw Mill River K.C., March 1968.

Ch. Eagle's Devil "D", winner of more than 20 all-breed Bests in Show, many Specialties and Group Firsts. Best of Breed at the Doberman Pinscher Club of America 1984 Specialty. With his handler, Carlos Rojas. This outstanding home-bred dog belongs to Dr. and Mrs. Anthony Di Nardo, East Hartford, Connecticut.

172

Bishop's Adoras Rocker, C.D.X., WAC, SchH 1, TT, here is winning at the Doberman Pinscher Club of America Specialty. Kay Martin, owner, Brooklyn, N.Y.

One of the lovely Doberman bitches owned by Dr. and Mrs. Anthony Di Nardo. This is Odessa.

quickly and with dexterity. The judge has a schedule to meet and only a few moments in which to evaluate each dog. You will immeasurably help yours to make a favorable impression if you are able to "get it all together" in a minimum amount of time. Practice at home before a mirror can be a great help toward bringing this about, facing the dog so that you see him from the same side that the judge will and working to make him look right in the shortest length of time.

Listen carefully as the judge describes the manner in which the dog is to be gaited, whether it is straight down and straight back; down the ring, across, and back; or in a triangle. The latter has become the most popular pattern with the majority of judges. "In a triangle" means the dog should move down the outer side of the ring to the first corner, across that end of the ring to the second corner, and then back to the judge from the second corner, using the center of the ring in a diagonal line. Please learn to do this pattern without breaking at each corner to twirl the dog around you, a senseless maneuver we sometimes have noted. Judges like to see the dog in an uninterrupted triangle, as they are thus able to get a better idea of the dog's gait.

It is impossible to overemphasize that the gait at which you move your dog is tremendously important, and considerable study and thought should be given to the matter. At home, have someone move the dog for you at different speeds so that you can tell which shows him off to best advantage. The most becoming action almost invariably is seen at a moderate gait, head up and topline holding. Do not gallop your dog around the ring or hurry him into a speed atypical of his breed. Nothing being rushed appears at its best; give your dog a chance to move along at his (and the breed's) natural gait. For a dog's action to be judged accurately, that dog should move with strength and power but not excessive speed, holding a straight line as he goes to and from the judge.

As you bring the dog back to the judge, stop him a few feet away and be sure that he is standing in a becoming position. Bait him to show the judge an alert expression, using whatever tasty morsel he has been trained to expect for this purpose or, if that works better for you, use a small squeak-toy in your hand. A reminder, please, to those using liver or treats. Take them with you when you leave the ring. Do not just drop them on the ground where they will be found by another dog.

When the awards have been made, accept yours graciously, no matter how you actually may feel about it. What's done is done, and arguing with a judge or stomping out of the ring is useless and a reflection on your sportsmanship. Be courteous, congratulate the winner if your dog was defeated, and try not to show your disappointment. By the same token, please be a gracious winner; this, surprisingly, sometimes seems to be still more difficult.

Doberman puppies outdoors for the first time survey the world through their fence. This is the first litter produced by Canadian and American Ch. Cherluck's Crimson 'n' Clover. Owned by Simca Kennels, Lana Sniderman and Bob Krol, Nobleton, Ontario.

Ch. Tarrado's Elegante owned by Mrs. David Berley, Heldervale Kennels, Slingerlands, N.Y. Robert S. Forsyth handler.

Chapter 13

Heredity and Inherited Characteristics of the Doberman

Once upon a time there was a monk named Gregor Johann Mendel. And this monk had a pea patch. After some time he noticed that he could predict the appearance of his peas. He then began certain cross-breeding experiments and found that he could predetermine the growth of green peas or yellow peas, wrinkled peas or smooth peas, tall pea plants and short pea plants. From this ordinary pea garden, he produced an extraordinary science—genetics. Mendel experimented with his peas and evolved the early theories of inheritance which so changed the course of biology, agriculture, medicine, and other related sciences. Of course, theories of heredity have progressed far beyond anything this simple monk could imagine; but it was his early experiments, unnoticed for many years, which touched off the revolution in the natural sciences.

Animal breeders were quick to use these theories in scientific breeding of purebred stock. Indeed, it is likely that many of them practiced scientific breeding without knowledge of scientific heredity. They bred like-to-like, bred dogs with favorable characteristics to obtain these traits in litters, and kept some records of bloodlines for mating purposes. They crossbred different types of dogs to encourage new traits. If they did not know just what it was that transmitted the desired features, they did know that somehow they were passed on to the young.

Good kennel management knows, however, that it is not enough to match up genes and chromosomes. This only transmits the raw material from dog to dog. The environment must also be proper. No matter how beautiful a dog's coat could be, if he isn't groomed and fed properly all his careful breeding will be lost. Therefore, modern breeders take advantage of modern science to breed scientifically, and then they take care of the dogs which result from these litters.

The Theory of Inheritance

There are many complex factors in inheritance, and modern geneticists are discovering more every day. Many things can influence the dog's breeding, but no outside interference can change his genetic structure, with the exception of accidental mutation.

In every living thing we find two types of cells: soma and germ. The somatic cells make up every part of the organism but one, the germ plasm which contains the germ cells. The germ plasm is the thin thread of our existence. Everything alive, from the lowliest amoeba to the dog and to man himself, is dependent for his uniqueness on germ plasm to perpetuate his kind.

Germ plasm in mammals is found in the sperm and eggs of the male and female. This substance contains tiny chemical entities called *genes*. Genes or groups of genes control the form and development of specific physical and mental characteristics. It may take several genes or combinations of genes to produce a certain appearance. For example, any number of genes may control the look of your dog's coat. There are genes to determine color, texture, length, and curliness (or lack of it). All of these factors can act together to produce the black, short-haired, hard-coated Doberman Pinscher.

The geneticist tells us that all the genes are found in every cell of the animal: *in pairs* everywhere but in the germ plasm. Even though every cell (other than germ plasm) has a specialized function—skin, muscles, heart, eye, and so on—the nucleus still has within it the genetic "fingerprint" of the complete animal.

When the somatic cells are dividing and redividing during the formation of the new animal, they divide so that each gene divides in half. Thus each somatic cell receives the same pair of genes. The germ plasm cells divide differently. They divide to form more cells, but each pair of genes divides in half (one-half the pair), either one gene or the other to each new cell. When the egg and the sperm, each made up of the special germ cells with only half the normal number of genes, unite, the genes again become paired. Each new individual inherits half his genes from each parent; but we cannot tell which half until

Brazilian Ch. Arabelle v Schloss, by Ch. Brazil v Marienburg ex Ch. Graca De Bela-
fonte. Breeder, V. Palumbo. Raul Lis Boa, owner.

181

International Ch. Elfred's Merri-Maker, by Ch. Steb's Top Skipper ex Ch. Barlynn's Clean Sweep, shown with handler Mrs. Ellen Hoffmann and judge John Lundberg.

after he has been born, although we can determine what kinds of characteristics he will inherit from the appearance and genetic makeup of his parents. Since many different combinations are possible, he will inherit characteristics different from those of his brothers and sisters; in fact, each individual is unique unto himself, although he will resemble his species closely.

The important thing to remember is that each characteristic is determined by a pair of genes. How does this work? Why will two black dogs, mated, produce a litter of all black dogs or litters with brown, tan, or blue dogs?

There are two types of genes: dominant and recessive. The dominant is the "stronger," you might say, and whenever it is present it overshadows the recessive or "weaker" gene. You can have a pair consisting of two dominant genes (purebred), two recessive genes (purebred), or a dominant and a recessive gene (hybrid). The recessive gene can show only if both the genes are recessive. But whenever one of the pair is a dominant gene, that characteristic will be the dominant one, although the recessive may show up some time later in another litter.

The light-colored dog at the extreme left is a blue Doberman Pinscher. Blue must be kept from becoming too light or grayish by proper selective breeding.

Let us say that "**B**" represents the dominant black color of the Doberman Pinscher coat color, and that "**b**" represents brown which is recessive in Dobermans. Each dog has two genes for his coat color. Since black is dominant over brown, whenever there is a **B** gene, the dog will be black. If the dog inherits a **B** gene from his father and a **B** gene from his mother he will be black and will pass only black genes to his children. But if the father with his **BB** genes mates with a bitch with **bb** genetic makeup (a brown color), the children will be black but will be capable of transmitting brown genes. This means that if one of these children mates with a Doberman with a **b** gene, brown *can* appear in *his* children. Simple listings of the combinations possible can enable any dog owner to see all the possible results of successive matings. It is by use of these Mendelian relations that the dog breeders control the quality of their dogs. Practically, it is difficult to see these effects when you only produce a litter or two, but the following variations are possible. These variations become very real when many litters are produced.

1. Two pure blacks mated will produce only purebred black dogs: **BB x BB = BB.**
2. Two purebred browns when mated will produce only brown (recessive) coated dogs: bb x bb = bb.
3. Two hybrids will produce some hybrids and some purebred dogs in the following ratios: Bb x Bb = BB, Bb, Bb, bb. This will show up as three black dogs and one brown dog.
4. A hybrid black and a purebred black will produce some purebred and some hybrid dogs, but they will all be black in appearance: **BB x Bb = BB, Bb, BB, Bb.**

One way of illustrating how the gene theory works is by boxes like the ones below:

Purebred Black (**BB**)   Hybrids (**Bb**)
  and brown (**bb**)

	b	b
B	Bb	Bb
B	Bb	Bb

	B	b
B	BB	Bb
b	bB	bb

184

Of course, in any single mating these expectations may not be realized, but once you have had many matings and litters you will see the patterns coming up. But since this theory is known, you need not take any chances. You can study the pedigrees and bloodlines of both male and female, and mate dogs which have characteristics you want. If you want brown Dobermans and you know the color is recessive, you must either mate purebred browns (**bb x bb**) or hybrids (**Bb x Bb**), or hybrid and purebred (**bb x Bb**). In the first case you can be sure of the color; in the second and third case there is only a chance you will obtain some browns.

Many people speak of a dog's bloodlines as if blood had something to do with inheritance. This is untrue. We should more properly talk of gene lines. Blood itself has nothing to do with inheritance. It is just one physical factor determined by genes.

People also thought that influences on the mother dog while she was pregnant would mark the puppies. We even know of people who think that if the mother listens to music, for example, while pregnant, that the child will have musical ability. Musical ability may run in the family, but this has nothing to do with playing the radio loudly during pregnancy.

Mutations and Abnormalities

This brings us to the problems of changes in types. There are persons who believe that if they clip the hair of their dog, if the dog is mated, the puppies will have shorter coats. This is utter nonsense, as you can see from the previous explanation. The length of a dog's coat is determined by his genetic makeup. Now if the breeder has been striving for shorter coats he can, using scientific methods, mate dogs which through some chance have coats which are shorter than average. Inbreeding and line-breeding will then fix this characteristic, and dogs will be born with shorter coats. In the case of the Doberman, the early dogs had long wavy coats, but this was deliberately bred out of them.

Occasionally there is a mutation in a breed. Genes are not immune to accident. Changes may come about chemically or from radiation (such as X-rays or nuclear particles) or some mix-up in the germ plasm. Sometimes chromosomes cross over and this changes the genetic makeup. These changes are sudden and quite rare. If the breeder wishes to keep one of these mutant changes he can try to duplicate it with inbreeding, but most mutations are downward on the evolutionary scale; only rarely is one an improvement.

How Heredity Affects Physical Characteristics and Behavior

Scientists and psychologists are still experimenting with animals to see just how an animal learns. Is a particular trait, such as scenting a trail, learned or inherited? The most we can say now is that certain tendencies run in families, and whether a pair of genes is responsible for this or it is learned through association is not yet clear. Psychologists do know that if they take a family of rats, let us say, which is very good at finding their way through a maze, the children of the family will learn to find their way in the maze more quickly than rats from another less talented family. If you take one of the rats away from its family and put it with another family which is not as adept, it will not learn to get through the maze; but if you put it back with its own family, it will learn more quickly than other rats might. Regardless of how a trait is acquired, family characteristics are most important, as dog breeders have discovered through their experience. Many examples are known.

Among all the bird-hunting breeds, the spaniels are the only ones which are bred to keep their noses close to the ground, hound fashion, when they hunt. Setters and pointers hunt with heads high. In crosses of Cockers and setters, the puppies all hunt with heads up, like setters. Even in crosses of setters with Bloodhounds the progeny were useless as trailing dogs. When you see a Cocker hunt with head carried high, he probably has some inherited characteristics of English Setter in him.

Some of the smaller breeds are natural tree dogs, and many make squirrel dogs *par excellence*, a use to which only those with shorter coats can be put. Some Poodles tree almost as well as tree hounds bred for this. This aptitude is not so well recognized as it should be, although it is by squirrel hunters.

While most persons never give posing much thought, observant breeders tell you how much easier it is to get certain dogs to pose as show dogs than others. There are many who will stand in a show pose when no hand is on or under them. This characteristic seems to run in families.

Gun-shyness also seems to run in families. Many dogs are also thunder-shy. It would appear best not to breed them, although it is possible to train these dogs so that they are not a total loss for hunting or retrieving.

The tendency to piddle is another characteristic which appears to be inherited. Unfortunately, it is often overlooked by breeders. There are too many dogs which panic when strangers or even their masters approach, and then wet. This is certainly most discouraging if your dog is a house dog and you want to preserve your rugs. It can be watched for and then eliminated by careful breeding.

All typical retrieving breeds love to retrieve; but there are strains where there is no interest, and retrieving can be trained into these dogs only with great difficulty. On the other hand, you can often see a leashed city-bred dog, familiar only with sparrows and pigeons, get out in a field and display a natural instinct for the art of retrieving. Careful breeding will help to preserve the hunting breeds and keep them from losing these instincts.

Natural retrievers just seem to have to have something to carry around in their mouths. One dog we know came to visit with his master and spent the entire afternoon carrying sticks of wood to the patio. By the end of the day we had a considerable pile of winter firewood, and we promptly invited our friend to come back again soon with his dog to complete the job. Many retrievers will even resort to picking up stools and carrying them around. If you have some old tennis balls around, you can discourage this filthy habit.

Some dogs can be taught easily to get the paper or the mail or even carry something in a bag.

Swimming is also another characteristic that seems to be inherited, although the natural tendency has to be encouraged by parent dogs which swim or owners who encourage swimming. Water dog retrievers have to know how to swim, but there is great variation among families and within breeds. If you want to hunt and own a dog which retrieves in water or live near water, you will want a dog with this characteristic.

The tendency to contract disease may be inherited. We know that certain tendencies run in human families, such as heart trouble and length of life. Back in the days when vaccines were not available and epidemics were rampant in animal families, it was seen that certain breeds did not have the same early symptoms of distemper as other dogs. Most dogs had convulsions when the temperature first started to rise, but Cockers and Poodles did not. Although mortality rates were the same, symptoms were not.

Doberman Pinschers are used extensively for police work and guard duty. Obviously, such a dog must have acute hearing, aggressiveness, and complete control. He must be easily trained in these areas. It would appear the better part of discretion to mate dogs with these characteristics if they run in families and to breed out those dogs

Ch. Marienburg's Lone Eagle, handled here by Moe Mujagawa for owners, Dr. and Mrs. Anthony Di Nardo, East Hartford, Connecticut. Lone Eagle was Number 2 Doberman in the Nation for 1978; 1979 Doberman Pinscher Club of America Top Twenty Winner; 1980 Number 1 Doberman Pinscher. A Best in Show winner, he has 151 Bests of Breed, including sixteen Specialty Shows. A sire par excellence, the best known of his sons is the great Ch. Eagle's Devil "D."

Damasyn The Waltzing Raven, by Damasyn The Solitaire, C.D.X. ex Damasyn The Winterwaltz, bred and owned by Joseph Rapisarda, is the dam of four champions.

which shy at gun fire, are poor trackers, or have limited intelligence and cannot learn quickly and reliably. Similarly, where there appears to be viciousness in the family inheritance, this should be bred out as fast as possible.

There is obviously much to be learned in this fascinating field of inheritance. Modern science has expanded and complicated Mendel's simple ideas which he learned in the pea patch, and still has far to go. We can predict the inheritance of physical characteristics such as color, shape, coat, skin, and so on, although we cannot always be absolutely sure of the results. With so many factors to consider (such as color, size, coat, and so on), the possible variations are almost infinite in the more complex mammals. As for inheriting or acquiring mental characteristics such as temperament, hunting ability, and tendencies for diseases, there is considerable disagreement among animal psychologists; but the consensus appears to be that the tendency to learn these traits is most likely inherited, but the traits themselves must be taught in some fashion.

The Mendelian theories of inheritance tell us how characteristics are passed from parents to children. But, as previously noted, the early experiments of Johann Mendel have been elaborated and modified by modern scientists. For more complex organisms, such as dogs, many genetic factors may be responsible for any one characteristic.

Coat Color

Theory tells us that we can predict that when two dogs with purebred black coats are mated, all of the resulting litter will have black coats. Similarly, brown-coated dogs mated together will produce only brown dogs. And we can also predict that dogs with hybrid black coats may very well produce both black and brown puppies.

But modern science has discovered also that the inheritance of color is more complicated. Colors occasionally blend or change as a result of the mixing of genes.

The ancient dog was probably a mixture of gray and brown, or derivations of black and yellow. All modern dogs have colorings which were originally possessed by their ancestors, passed down and modified by accidental or deliberate breeding.

The color and markings of the Doberman Pinscher have been carefully bred and maintained. The basic color is the result of the density

Ch. Taina vom Ahrtal, by Ch. Felix vom Ahrtal ex Iduna vom Ahrtal, bred and handled here by Tess Henseler under judge Chris Shuttleworth (*left*). Owner is Evelyn L. Ahr.

Ch. Felix vom Ahrtal, by Ch. Lakecrest's Thunderstorm ex Ch. Willa v. Ahrtal, bred and owned by Tess Henseler who is shown handling the champ under judge Carl Seishab *(left)*.

of color pigments in the skin and hair. The denser the black pigments, the darker the coat color. Less density produces brown, blue, or fawn. Of course, genes are responsible for the density.

One of the problems of breeding for darker and more richly marked dogs is a condition called "melanism." This is a progressive blackening which gradually erases markings or causes them to become muddy and indistinct. The result of this overbreeding can be seen in the Manchester Black-and-Tan Terrier. When it happens to the Doberman, the markings disappear and, as a result, the face takes on a rather unpleasant expression.

The opposite of melanism is a condition caused by less dense pigmentation which often produces fawn or light-colored dogs. (The extreme is a complete lack of pigment or albinism.)

It would appear that blue coat color is a variation of black, though some breeders believe that it comes from a breakdown of the recessive brown color.

Breeders, therefore, when breeding for more attractive colorings and markings,must aim for certain standards.Dobermans bred for black coats and rich red markings must not be permitted to become too dark and muddied. This is accomplished by occasionally mixing blacks and browns or hybrids instead of always breeding purebred blacks to each other.

Brown dogs are best if the brown remains a medium color with rich markings. There are many shades of brown, but the darker tones tend to obscure the markings and the very light colors may become silvery grays. Blues must be kept from becoming too light or grayish.

One of the problems of breeders is maintaining the rich markings of the Doberman while discouraging any white on the chest. The A.K.C. standard allows for only ½ square inch of white. More than that is disallowed in the show ring. Dogs which tend to pass this white down to their offspring are not popular as sires or dams no matter how excellent their other qualities.

Not only do the markings reflect the basic coat color but also the eyes, lips, and nose. The darker the coat, the darker the color of the eyes. Dark brown eyes are the ideal, but browns and blues may have lighter eyes. Very light eyes (hawkeyes) should be bred out.

Similarly, the nose reflects the coat color. Black dogs generally have black noses, brown dogs have brown noses, and the blues have grayish noses. Sometimes a flesh-colored nose or even a butterfly nose (varied pigmentation) appears, but this can be eliminated in later breedings. Eyelids, lips, and inner ear are also pigmented in close relationship with coat color.

Size

The A.K.C. standard specifies that male Dobermans must measure between 26 and 28″, 27½″ being the ideal height. Bitches are slightly smaller, 24 to 26″, 25½″ being ideal. A dog's height is measured at the withers.

The size of a dog can determine his usefulness. After all, although a toy dog may sound like ten dogs if he is yapping loud enough, he is only one very small dog. The medium size of the powerful Doberman makes him ideal as a watchdog. Apartment dwellers are especially grateful for this. He is large enough to be useful, but small enough not to crowd the family.

In use as a working dog his size is also an asset. Many large dogs are not speedy or agile enough to be efficient.

Temperament

Animal behaviorists and geneticists are not sure whether certain traits of behavior characteristics are inherited or not, and this is still being investigated. We do know that the best of dogs (from a genetic

Canadian Ch. Shiroya's Scarlett Petticoat had eleven points including both majors as of May 1982. This quality bitch owned by Kathleen Daily is pictured here with judge Robert S. Forsyth.

Buy a special toy for your Doberman, or better yet get Nylabone® , a product that is safe and satisfies a dog's chewing needs.

standpoint) can be ruined by improper training and care, and a relatively unpromising dog can certainly become a faithful and loving pet if he is treated well.

In the case of the Doberman, rumors have spread that he is dangerous or temperamental. This probably arises because of his work as a war or police dog. Anyone who has faced one of these dogs doing his job may be inclined to say that the Doberman is aggressive. What he may have failed to note is that the dog is completely under control. He does only what his master orders him to do.

But the ability to patrol a store or a battlefront requires certain traits: a keen sense of smell (for tracking), fearlessness and alertness, devotion to his master. You may not know it, but your Doberman is one of the fastest dogs in the canine world.

The Doberman appears to be a "born" watchdog. He can be taught to guard a home and protect children and property.

Does this sound like all work and no play for our dog? Not at all. The Doberman loves nothing better than a good romp with his master or the children. In fact he takes a lot of abuse from "his" youngsters. We should remind you here that children should be taught not to tease or hurt a dog when they are playing. We remember watching in horror as a small child practically pulled the ears off his family dog. The dog let out an occasional whimper and finally ran off, but he didn't so much as growl at his younger master (and tormentor). This was certainly the case of a well-trained dog and a poorly trained child.

Moreover, a Doberman is generally a peaceful dog. Left alone by other dogs he goes his way. But woe betide the dog who attacks him!

The Doberman is fearless, alert, and keen-sensed, and he makes an excellent watchdog. In addition he is protective of his master and his master's family and property. All these qualities, with careful training, can be used by families who want a pet or the police or armed services who want a working dog. Fortunately, breeders have recognized this and tend to preserve this as a desirable characteristic. They realize that a handsome dog is a joy to look at, but a dog's character is equally important and they have taken care to preserve the Doberman's unique heritage.

English Ch. Tavery's Stormy Wrath, owned by Mrs. J. Curnow.

Ch. Votan v Gruenewald II, by Ch. Dictator von Glenhugel ex Ch. Hanschen v Gruenewald. Bred by Earl Spicer and owned by Willie Deckert.

Ch. Majakens Bronze Erick, bred and owned by James G. Kennedy, shown with handler Marlene Kennedy and judge Mr. Adair.

Appearance

The best way to judge a dog's appearance is to compare him with the A.K.C. standard.

In physique the Doberman appears muscular and powerful. But the quality which attracts most people is the Doberman's elegant, proud appearance and handsome coloring. There is almost a noble look as he stands there, compact, sturdy, ears alert, eyes shining.

Early pictures of the Doberman show a dog with a somewhat heavier, coarser look. The coat is thick and wavy, the muzzle coarse. Breeders with foresight must have pictured to themselves the Doberman of today and bred toward that ideal.

As an example, the head of the early Doberman was different from today's, and it is still subject to variation. The older Dobermans had head types more resembling the Rottweiler, with heavy jowls and thick skulls. Gradually, the skull became longer so that today's dog can be classified as a long-headed breed. More value is obviously being placed on the shape of the head than in earlier days. Time will probably fix the size and shape more surely.

As the length of the head was changed, other parts altered too. A ridge appeared from the middle of the frontal bone to the temples. This was necessary for anchoring the jaw muscles, for as the head elongated, these muscles had to be moved and the ridge became more noticeable. Thus we see both Nature and the breeder cooperating for a better, handsomer animal.

Life Span

Most dogs live to a ripe old age if given proper care. The Methuselahs of the dog world may even reach eighteen or twenty years of age, and twelve or fourteen is about average. The Doberman, a naturally robust type, should have many years of useful life, but thirteen is a good average.

Ch. Fidelia vom Ahrtal, bred and owned by Tess Henseler.

Chapter 14

Breeding Your Doberman

The Doberman Brood Bitch

We have in an earlier chapter discussed selection of a bitch you plan to use for breeding. In making this important purchase, you will be choosing a bitch who you hope will become the foundation of your kennel. Thus she must be of the finest producing bloodlines, excellent in temperament, of good type, and free of major faults or unsoundness. If you are offered a "bargain" brood bitch, be wary, as for this purchase you should not settle for less than the best and the price will be in accordance with the quality.

Conscientious breeders feel quite strongly that the only possible reason for producing puppies is the ambition to improve and uphold quality and temperament within the breed—definitely *not* because one hopes to make a quick cash profit on a mediocre litter, which never seems to work out that way in the long run and which accomplishes little beyond perhaps adding to the nation's heartbreaking number of unwanted canines. The only reason ever for breeding a litter is, with conscientious people, a desire to improve the quality of dogs in their own kennel or, as pet owners, because they wish to add to the number of dogs they themselves own with a puppy or two from their present favorites. In either case breeding should not take place unless one has definitely prospective owners for as many puppies as the litter may contain, lest you find yourself with several fast-growing young dogs and no homes in which to place them.

Bitches should not be mated earlier than their second season, by which time they should be from fifteen to eighteen months old. Many breeders prefer to wait and first finish the championships of their show bitches before breeding them, as pregnancy can be a disaster to a show coat and getting the bitch back in shape again takes time. When you have decided what will be the proper time, start watching at least several months ahead for what you feel would be the perfect mate to best complement your bitch's quality and bloodlines Subscribe to the magazines which feature your breed exclusively and to some which cover all breeds in order to familiarize yourself with outstanding stud dogs in areas other than your own for there is no necessity nowadays to limit your choice to a nearby dog unless you truly like him and feel that he is the most suitable. It is quite usual to ship a bitch to a stud dog a distance away, and this generally works out with no ill effects. The important thing is that you need a stud dog strong in those features where your bitch is weak or lacking and of bloodlines compatible to hers. Compare the background of both your bitch and the stud dog under consideration, paying particular attention to the quality of the puppies from bitches with backgrounds similar to your bitch's. If the puppies have been of the type and quality you admire, then this dog would seem a sensible choice for yours, too.

Stud fees may be a few hundred dollars, sometimes even more under special situations for a particularly successful sire. It is money well spent, however. Do *not* ever breed to a dog because he is less expensive than the others unless you honestly believe that he can sire the kind of puppies who will be a credit to your kennel and your breed.

Contacting the owners of the stud dogs you find interesting will bring you pedigrees and pictures which you can then study in relation to your bitch's pedigree and conformation. Discuss your plans with other breeders who are knowledgeable (including the one who bred your own bitch). You may not always receive an entirely unbiased opinion (particularly if the person giving it also has an available stud dog), but one learns by discussion so listen to what they say, consider their opinions, and then you may be better qualified to form your own opinion.

As soon as you have made a choice, phone the owner of the stud dog you wish to use to find out if this will be agreeable. You will be asked about the bitch's health, soundness, temperament, and freedom from serious faults. A copy of her pedigree may be requested, as might a picture of her. A discussion of her background over the telephone may be sufficient to assure the stud's owner that she is suitable for the stud dog and of type, breeding, and quality herself to produce puppies of the quality for which the dog is noted. The owner of a top-quality stud is often extremely selective in the bitches permitted to be bred to his dog, in an effort to keep the standard of his puppies high. The owner of a stud dog may require that the bitch be tested for brucellosis, which should be attended to not more than a month previous to the breeding.

Check out which airport will be most convenient for the person meeting and returning the bitch if she is to be shipped and also what airlines use that airport. You will find that the airlines are also apt to have special requirements concerning acceptance of animals for shipping. These include weather limitations and types of crates which are acceptable. The weather limits have to do with extreme heat and extreme cold at the point of destination, as some airlines will not fly dogs into temperatures above or below certain levels, fearing for their safety. The crate problem is a simple one, since if your own crate is not suitable, most of the airlines have specially designed crates available for purchase at a fair and moderate price. It is a good plan to purchase one of these if you intend to be shipping dogs with any sort of frequency. They are made of fiberglass and are the safest type to use for shipping.

Normally you must notify the airline several days in advance to make a reservation, as they are able to accommodate only a certain number of dogs on each flight. Plan on shipping the bitch on about her eighth or ninth day of season, but be careful to avoid shipping her on a weekend, when schedules often vary and freight offices are apt to be closed. Whenever you can, ship your bitch on a direct flight. Changing planes always carries a certain amount of risk of a dog being overlooked or wrongly routed at the middle stop, so avoid this danger if at all possible. The bitch must be accompanied by a health certificate which you must obtain from your veterinarian before taking her to the airport. Usually it will be necessary to have the bitch at the airport about two hours prior to flight time. Before finalizing arrangements, find out from the stud's owner at what time of day it will be most convenient to have the bitch picked up promptly upon arrival.

It is simpler if you can plan to bring the bitch to the stud dog. Some people feel that the trauma of the flight may cause the bitch to not conceive; and, of course, undeniably there is a slight risk in shipping which can be avoided if you are able to drive the bitch to her destination. Be sure to leave yourself sufficient time to assure your arrival at the right time for her for breeding (normally the tenth to fourteenth day following the first signs of color); and remember that if you want the bitch bred twice, you should allow a day to elapse between the two matings. Do not expect the stud's owner to house you while you are there. Locate a nearby motel that takes dogs and make that your headquarters.

Just prior to the time your bitch is due in season, you should take her to visit your veterinarian. She should be checked for worms and should receive all the booster shots for which she is due plus one for parvo virus, unless she has had the latter shot fairly recently. The brucellosis test can also be done then, and the health certificate can be obtained for shipping if she is to travel by air. Should the bitch be at all overweight, now is the time to get the surplus off. She should be in good condition, neither underweight nor overweight, at the time of breeding.

The moment you notice the swelling of the vulva, for which you should be checking daily as the time for her season approaches, and the appearance of color, immediately contact the stud's owner and settle on the day for shipping or make the appointment for your arrival with the bitch for breeding. If you are shipping the bitch, the stud fee check should be mailed immediately, leaving ample time for it to have been received when the bitch arrives and the mating takes place. Be sure to call the airline making her reservation at that time, too.

Do not feed the bitch within a few hours before shipping her. Be certain that she has had a drink of water and been well exercised before closing her in the crate. Several layers of newspapers, topped with some shredded newspaper, make a good bed and can be discarded when she arrives at her destination; these can be replaced with fresh newspapers for her return home. Remember that the bitch should be brought to the airport about two hours before flight time as sometimes the airlines refuse to accept late arrivals.

If you are taking your bitch by car, be certain that you will arrive at a reasonable time of day. Do not appear late in the evening. If your arrival in town is not until late, get a good night's sleep at your motel and contact the stud's owner first thing in the morning. If possible, leave children and relatives at home, as they will only be in the way and perhaps unwelcome by the stud's owner. Most stud dog owners prefer not to have any unnecessary people on hand during the actual mating.

After the breeding has taken place, if you wish to sit and visit for awhile and the stud's owner has the time, return the bitch to her crate

Opposite page: Stolz Meadow Rue v Obsidian, C.D.X., by Civetta's Bruin of Kami ex Civetta's Obsidian, U.D., WAC. Owner-handled by Kay Martin, Brooklyn, N.Y.

in your car (first ascertaining, of course, that the temperature is comfortable for her and that there is proper ventilation). She should not be permitted to urinate for at least one hour following the breeding. This is the time when you get the business part of the transaction attended to. Pay the stud fee, upon which you should receive your breeding certificate and, if you do not already have it, a copy of the stud dog's pedigree. The owner of the stud dog does not sign or furnish a litter registration application until the puppies have been born.

Upon your return home, you can settle down and plan in happy anticipation a wonderful litter of puppies. A word of caution! Remember that although she has been bred, your bitch is still an interesting target for all male dogs, so guard her carefully for the next week or until you are absolutely certain that her season has entirely ended. This would be no time to have any unfortunate incident with another dog.

When breeding some bitches, it may be necessary to muzzle them. Select a muzzle that is secure and comfortable.

The compatibility of prospective breeders should be ascertained before breeding can take place. A successful mating is hardly possible between belligerent and aggressive partners.

The Doberman Stud Dog

Choosing the best stud dog to complement your bitch is often very difficult. The two principal factors to be considered should be the stud's conformation and his pedigree. Conformation is fairly obvious; you want a dog that is typical of the breed in the words of the standard of perfection. Understanding pedigrees is a bit more subtle since the pedigree lists the ancestry of the dog and involves individuals and bloodlines with which you may not be entirely familiar.

To a novice in the breed, then, the correct interpretation of a pedigree may at first be difficult to grasp. Study the pictures and text of this book and you will find many names of important bloodlines and members of the breed. Also make an effort to discuss the various dogs behind the proposed stud with some of the more experienced breeders, starting with the breeder of your own bitch. Frequently these folks will be personally familiar with many of the dogs in question, can offer opinions of them, and may have access to additional pictures which you would benefit by seeing.

It is very important that the stud's pedigree should be harmonious with that of the bitch you plan on breeding to him. Do not rush out and breed to the latest winner with no thought of whether or not he can produce true quality. By no means are all great show dogs great producers. It is the producing record of the dog in question and the dogs and bitches from which he has come which should be the basis on which you make your choice.

Breeding dogs is never a money-making operation. By the time you pay a stud fee, care for the bitch during pregnancy, whelp the litter, and rear the puppies through their early shots, worming, and so on, you will be fortunate to break even financially once the puppies have been sold. Your chances of doing this are greater if you are breeding for a show-quality litter which will bring you higher prices as the pups are sold as show prospects. Therefore, your wisest investment is to use the best dog available for your bitch regardless of the cost; then you should wind up with more valuable puppies. Remember that it is equally costly to raise mediocre puppies as top ones, and your chances of financial return are better on the latter. To breed to the most excellent, most suitable stud dog you can find is the only sensible thing to do, and it is poor economy to quibble over the amount you are paying in stud fee.

It will be your decision which course you decide to follow when you breed your bitch, as there are three options: line-breeding, inbreeding, and outcrossing. Each of these methods has its supporters and its detractors! Line-breeding is breeding a bitch to a dog belonging originally to the same canine family, being descended from the same ancestors, such as half-brother to half-sister, grandsire to granddaughters, niece to uncle (and vice-versa) or cousin to cousin. Inbreeding is breeding father to daughter, mother to son, or full brother to sister. Outcross breeding is breeding a dog and a bitch with no or only a few mutual ancestors.

Line-breeding is probably the safest course, and the one most likely to bring results, for the novice breeder. The more sophisticated inbreeding should be left to the experienced, long-time breeders who thoroughly know and understand the risks and the possibilities involved with a particular line. It is usually done in an effort to intensify some ideal feature in that strain. Outcrossing is the reverse of inbreeding, an effort to introduce improvement in a specific feature needing correction, such as a shorter back, better movement, more correct head or coat, and so on.

It is the serious breeder's ambition to develop a strain or bloodline of their own, one strong in qualities for which their dogs will become distinguished. However, it must be realized that this will involve time, patience, and at least several generations before the achievement can be claimed. The safest way to embark on this plan, as we have mentioned, is by the selection and breeding of one or two bitches, the best you can buy and from top-producing kennels. In the beginning you do *not* really have to own a stud dog. In the long run it is less expensive and sounder judgment to pay a stud fee when you are ready to breed a bitch than to purchase a stud dog and feed him all year; a stud dog does not win any popularity contests with owners of bitches to be bred until he becomes a champion, has been successfully Specialed for awhile, and has been at least moderately advertised, all of which adds up to a quite healthy expenditure.

The wisest course for the inexperienced breeder just starting out in dogs is as outlined above. Keep the best bitch puppy from the first several litters. After that you may wish to consider keeping your own stud dog if there has been a particularly handsome male in one of your litters that you feel has great potential or if you know where there is one available that you are interested in, with the feeling that he would work in nicely with the breeding program on which you have embarked. By this time, with several litters already born, your eye should have developed to a point enabling you to make a wise choice, either from one of your own litters or from among dogs you have seen that appear suitable.

The greatest care should be taken in the selection of your own stud dog. He must be of true type and highest quality as he may be responsible for siring many puppies each year, and he should come from a line of excellent dogs on both sides of his pedigree which themselves are, and which are descended from, successful producers. This dog should have no glaring faults in conformation; he should be of such quality that he can hold his own in keenest competition within his breed. He should be in good health, be virile and be a keen stud dog, a proven sire able to transmit his correct qualities to his puppies. Such a dog will be enormously expensive unless you have the good fortune to produce him in one of your own litters. To buy and use a lesser stud dog, however, is downgrading your breeding program unnecessarily since there are so many dogs fitting the description of a fine stud whose services can be used on payment of a stud fee.

You should *never* breed to an unsound dog or one with any serious standard or disqualifying faults. Not all champions by any means pass

along their best features; and by the same token, occasionally you will find a great one who can pass along his best features but never gained his championship title due to some unusual circumstances. The information you need about a stud dog is what type of puppies he has produced and with what bloodlines and whether or not he possesses the bloodlines and attributes considered characteristic of the best in your breed.

If you go out to buy a stud dog, obviously he will not be a puppy but rather a fully mature and proven male with as many of the best attributes as possible. True, he will be an expensive investment, but if you choose and make his selection with care and forethought, he may well prove to be one of the best investments you have ever made.

Of course, the most exciting of all is when a young male you have decided to keep from one of your litters due to his tremendous show potential turns out to be a stud dog such as we have described. In this case he should be managed with care, for he is a valuable property that can contribute inestimably to this breed as a whole and to your own kennel specifically.

Do not permit your stud dog to be used until he is about a year old, and even then he should be bred to a mature, proven matron accustomed to breeding who will make his first experience pleasant and easy. A young dog can be put off forever by a maiden bitch who fights and resists his advances. Never allow this to happen. Always start a stud dog out with a bitch who is mature, has been bred previously, and is of even temperament. The first breeding should be performed in quiet surroundings with only you and one other person to hold the bitch. Do not make it a circus, as the experience will determine the dog's outlook about future stud work. If he does not enjoy the first experience or associates it with any unpleasantness, you may well have a problem in the future.

Your young stud must permit help with the breeding, as later there will be bitches who will not be cooperative. If right from the beginning you are there helping him and praising him whether or not your assistance is actually needed, he will expect and accept this as a matter of course when a difficult bitch comes along.

Opposite page: Ch. Civetteta's Wolf Whistle of Kami, C.D.X., ROM, owner-handled by Kay Martin, Brooklyn, N.Y. winning the Working Group at Westbury K.A. In 1973, judged by Robert S. Salomon.

The well-known winner Glenayr Jamison, by Ch. Glenayr Dufferinand ex Tedell Taras Harp was bred by Richard and Barbara Duklis and is owned by Jay-Mee's Dobbies, San Juan, Puerto Rico. Best of Breed in the Venezuelan International in 1982 under judge Richard Guevara.

Ch. Encore's Black Rites, Don V. Simmons handler, winning the Stud Dog Class at the Quaker City Doberman Pinscher Club Specialty.

Things to have handy before introducing your dog and the bitch are K-Y jelly (the only lubricant which should be used) and a length of gauze with which to muzzle the bitch should it be necessary to keep her from biting you or the dog. Some bitches put up a fight; others are calm. It is best to be prepared.

At the time of the breeding the stud fee comes due, and it is expected that it will be paid promptly. Normally a return service is offered in case the bitch misses or fails to produce one live puppy. Conditions of the service are what the stud dog's owner makes them, and there are no standard rules covering this. The stud fee is paid for the act, not the result. If the bitch fails to conceive, it is customary for the owner to offer a free return service; but this is a courtesy and not to be considered a right, particularly in the case of a proven stud who is siring consistently and whose fault the failure obviously is *not*. Stud dog owners are always anxious to see their clients get good value and to have in the ring winning young stock by their dog; therefore, very few refuse to mate the second time. It is wise, however, for both parties to have the terms of the transaction clearly understood at the time of the breeding.

If the return service has been provided and the bitch has missed a second time, that is considered to be the end of the matter and the owner would be expected to pay a further fee if it is felt that the bitch should be given a third chance with the stud dog. The management of a stud dog and his visiting bitches is quite a task, and a stud fee has usually been well earned when one service has been achieved, let alone by repeated visits from the same bitch.

The accepted litter is one live puppy. It is wise to have printed a breeding certificate which the owner of the stud dog and the owner of the bitch both sign. This should list in detail the conditions of the breeding as well as the dates of the mating.

Upon occasion, arrangements other than a stud fee in cash are made for a breeding, such as the owner of the stud taking a pick-of-the-litter puppy in lieu of money. This should be clearly specified on the breeding certificate along with the terms of the age at which the stud's owner will select the puppy, whether it is to be a specific sex, or whether it is to be the pick of the entire litter.

The price of a stud fee varies according to circumstances. Usually, to prove a young stud dog, his owner will allow the first breeding to be quite inexpensive. Then, once a bitch has become pregnant by him, he becomes a "proven stud" and the fee rises accordingly for bitches that follow. The sire of championship-quality puppies will bring a stud fee of at least the purchase price of one show puppy as the accepted "rule-of-thumb." Until at least one champion by your stud dog has finished, the fee will remain equal to the price of one pet puppy. When his list of champions starts to grow, so does the amount of the stud fee. For a top-producing sire of champions, the stud fee will rise accordingly.

Almost invariably it is the bitch who comes to the stud dog for the breeding. Immediately upon having selected the stud dog you wish to use, discuss the possibility with the owner of that dog. It is the stud dog owner's prerogative to refuse to breed any bitch deemed un-suitable for this dog. Stud fee and method of payment should be stated

The whelping box keeps the mother and her litter together in comfort in one safe place.

at this time, and a decision reached on whether it is to be a full cash transaction at the time of the mating or a pick-of-the-litter puppy, usually at eight weeks of age.

If the owner of the stud dog must travel to an airport to meet the bitch and ship her for the flight home, an additional charge will be made for time, tolls, and gasoline based on the stud owner's proximity to the airport. The stud fee includes board for the day on the bitch's arrival through two days for breeding, with a day in between. If it is necessary that the bitch remain longer, it is very likely that additional board will be charged at the normal per-day rate for the breed.

Be sure to advise the stud's owner as soon as you know that your bitch is in season so that the stud dog will be available. This is especially important because if he is a dog being shown, he and his owner may be unavailable owing to the dog's absence from home.

As the owner of a stud dog being offered to the public, it is essential that you have proper facilities for the care of visiting bitches. Nothing can be worse than a bitch being insecurely housed and slipping out to become lost or bred by the wrong dog. If you are taking people's valued bitches into your kennel or home, it is imperative that you provide them with comfortable, secure housing and good care while they are your responsibility.

There is no dog more valuable than the proven sire of champions, Group winners, and Best in Show dogs. Once you have such an animal, guard his reputation well and do *not* permit him to be bred to just any bitch that comes along. It takes two to make the puppies; even the most dominant stud can not do it all himself, so never permit him to breed a bitch you consider unworthy. Remember that when the puppies arrive, it will be your stud dog who will be blamed for any lack of quality, while the bitch's shortcomings will be quickly and conveniently overlooked.

Going into the actual management of the mating is a bit superfluous here. If you have had previous experience in breeding a dog and bitch you will know how the mating is done. If you do not have such experience, you should not attempt to follow directions given in a book but should have a veterinarian, breeder friend, or handler there to help you the first few times. You do not just turn the dog and bitch loose together and await developments, as too many things can go wrong and you may altogether miss getting the bitch bred. Someone should hold the dog and the bitch (one person each) until the "tie" is made and these two people should stay with them during the entire act.

214

Ch. Damasyn The Solitaire, C.D.X., by Ch. Dictator von Glenhugel ex Ch. Damasyn The Sultry Sister, owned by Mrs. Bob Adamson. This excellent Doberman is sire of fourteen champions, including the first American Grand Victor, Ch. Berman Brier.

Ch. Bailes Bigwig of Gracewood, bred and owned by Mrs. Boyce Bailes, with judge Percy Roberts holding ribbon.

Elfred's Mr. Victory, by Tri-International Ch. Elfred's Spark Plug ex K. L's Hella, bred by Mrs. Ellen Hoffmann and owned by Mr. C.A. Bodar, shown here being handled by Mrs. Ellen Hoffmann while judge Carl Woods looks on.

If you get a complete tie, probably only the one mating is absolutely necessary. However, especially with a maiden bitch or one that has come a long distance for this breeding, we prefer following up with a second breeding, leaving one day in between the two matings. In this way there will be little or no chance of the bitch missing.

Once the tie has been completed and the dogs release, be certain that the male's penis goes completely back within its sheath. He should be allowed a drink of water and a short walk, and then he should be put into his crate or somewhere alone where he can settle down. Do not allow him to be with other dogs for a while as they will notice the odor of the bitch on him, and particularly with other males present, he may become involved in a fight.

Pregnancy, Whelping, and the Litter

Once the bitch has been bred and is back at home, remember to keep an ever watchful eye that no other male gets to her until at least the twenty-second day of her season has passed. Until then, it will still be possible for an unwanted breeding to take place, which at this point would be catastrophic. Remember that she actually can have two separate litters by two different dogs, so take care.

In other ways, she should be treated normally. Controlled exercise is good, and necessary for the bitch throughout her pregnancy, tapering it off to just several short walks daily, preferably on lead, as she reaches about her seventh week. As her time grows close, be careful about her jumping or playing too roughly.

The theory that a bitch should be overstuffed with food when pregnant is a poor one. A fat bitch is never an easy whelper, so the overfeeding you consider good for her may well turn out to be the exact opposite. During the first few weeks of pregnancy, your bitch should be fed her normal diet. At four to five weeks along, calcium should be added to her food. At seven weeks her food may be increased if she seems to crave more than she is getting, and a meal of canned milk (mixed with an equal amount of water) should be introduced. If she is fed just once a day, add another meal rather than overload her with too much at one time. If twice a day is her schedule, then a bit more food can be added to each feeding.

A week before the pups are due, your bitch should be introduced to her whelping box so that she will be accustomed to it and feel at home there when the puppies arrive. She should be encouraged to sleep

Ch. Berman Bangles, by Ch. Damasyn The Solitaire, C.D.X. ex Berman Armina, owned and bred by Bernard Berman who is shown handling this champion.

there but permitted to come and go as she wishes. The box should be roomy enough for her to lie down and stretch out but not too large lest the pups have more room than is needed in which to roam and possibly get chilled by going too far away from their mother. Be sure that the box has a "pig rail"; this will prevent the puppies from being crushed against the sides. The room in which the box is placed, either in your home or in the kennel, should be kept at about 70 degrees Fahrenheit. In winter it may be necessary to have an infrared lamp over the whelping box, in which case be careful not to place it too low or close to the puppies.

218

Newspapers will become a very important commodity, so start collecting them well in advance to have a big pile handy to the whelping box. With a litter of puppies, one never seems to have papers enough, so the higher pile to start with, the better off you will be. Other necessities for whelping time are clean, soft turkish towels, scissors, and a bottle of alcohol.

You will know that her time is very near when your bitch becomes restless, wandering in and out of her box and of the room. She may refuse food, and at that point her temperature will start to drop. She will dig at and tear up the newspapers in her box, shiver, and generally look uncomfortable. Only you should be with your bitch at this time. She does not need spectators; and several people, even though they may be family members whom she knows, hanging over her may upset her to the point where she may harm the puppies. You should remain nearby, quietly watching, not fussing or hovering; speak calmly and frequently to her to instill confidence. Eventually she will settle down in her box and begin panting; contractions will follow. Soon thereafter a puppy will start to emerge, sliding out with the contractions. The mother immediately should open the sac, sever the cord with her teeth, and then clean up the puppy. She will also eat the placenta, which you should permit. Once the puppy is cleaned, it should be placed next to the bitch unless she is showing signs of having the next one immediately. Almost at once the puppy will start looking for a nipple on which to nurse, and you should ascertain that it is able to latch on successfully.

If the puppy is a breech (*i.e.*, born feet first), you must watch carefully for it to be completely delivered as quickly as possible and the sac removed quickly so that the puppy does not drown. Sometimes even a normally positioned birth will seem extremely slow in coming. Should this occur, you might take a clean towel and, as the bitch contracts, pull the puppy out, doing so gently and with utmost care. If, once the puppy is delivered, it shows little signs of life, take a rough turkish towel and massage the puppy's chest by rubbing quite briskly back and forth. Continue this for about fifteen minutes, and be sure that the mouth is free from liquid. It may be necessary to try mouth-to-mouth breathing, which is done by pressing the puppy's jaws open and, using a finger, depressing the tongue which may be stuck to the roof of the mouth. Then place your mouth against the puppy's and blow hard down the puppy's throat. Bubbles may pop out of its nose, but keep on blowing. Rub the puppy's chest with the towel again and try artificial respiration, pressing the sides of the chest together slowly and rhythmically—in and out, in and out. Keep trying one method or the other for at least twenty minutes before giving up. You may be rewarded with a live puppy who otherwise would not have made it.

If you are successful in bringing the puppy around, do not immediately put it back with the mother as it should be kept extra warm. Put it in a cardboard box on an electric heating pad or, if it is the time of year when your heat is running, near a radiator or near the fireplace or stove. As soon as the rest of the litter has been born it then can join the others.

An hour or more may elapse between puppies, which is fine so long as the bitch seems comfortable and is neither straining nor contracting. She should not be permitted to remain unassisted for more than an hour if she does continue to contract. This is when you should get her to your veterinarian, whom you should already have alerted to the possibility of a problem existing. He should examine her and perhaps give her a shot of Pituitrin. In some cases the veterinarian may find that a Caesarean section is necessary due to a puppy being lodged in a manner making normal delivery impossible. Sometimes this is caused by an abnormally large puppy, or it may just be that the puppy is simply turned in the wrong position. If the bitch does require a Caesarean section, the puppies already born must be kept warm in their cardboard box with a heating pad under the box.

Once the section is done, get the bitch and the puppies home. Do not attempt to put the puppies in with the bitch until she has regained consciousness as she may unknowingly hurt them. But do get them back to her as soon as possible for them to start nursing.

Should the mother lack milk at this time, the puppies must be fed by hand, kept very warm, and held onto the mother's teats several times a day in order to stimulate and encourage the secretion of milk, which should start shortly.

Assuming that there has been no problem and that the bitch has whelped naturally, you should insist that she go out to exercise, staying just long enough to make herself comfortable. She can be offered a bowl of milk and a biscuit, but then she should settle down with her family. Freshen the whelping box for her with fresh newspapers while she is taking this respite so that she and the puppies will have a clean bed.

Unless some problem arises, there is little you must do about the puppies until they become three to four weeks old. Keep the box clean and supplied with fresh newspapers the first few days, but then

Ch. Stromson's Crashing Baron Jet, by Ch. Rancho Dobe's Storm, bred by Betty Louise Van Bueltzen and owned by Mary D. and Walter J. Quinn. Judge Paul T. Hakel presents ribbon while William P. Gilbert handled the winner.

Grand Champion Juon with three of his children. Mr. and Mrs. Mulero, Dompierre/Mer, France.

turkish towels should be tacked down to the bottom of the box so that the puppies will have traction as they move about.

If the bitch has difficulties with her milk supply, or if you should be so unfortunate as to lose her, then you must be prepared to either hand-feed or tube-feed the puppies if they are to survive. We personally prefer tube-feeding as it is so much faster and easier. If the bitch is available, it is best that she continues to clean and care for the puppies in the normal manner excepting for the food supplements you will provide. If it is impossible for her to do this, then after every feeding you must gently rub each puppy's abdomen with wet cotton to make it urinate, and the rectum should be gently rubbed to open the bowels.

Newborn puppies must be fed every three to four hours around the clock. The puppies must be kept warm during this time. Have your veterinarian teach you how to tube-feed. You will find that it is really quite simple.

222

After a normal whelping, the bitch will require additional food to enable her to produce sufficient milk. In addition to being fed twice daily, she should be given some canned milk several times each day.

When the puppies are two weeks old, their nails should be clipped, as they are needle sharp at this age and can hurt or damage the mother's teats and stomach as the pups hold on to nurse.

Between three and four weeks of age, the puppies should begin to be weaned. Scraped beef (prepared by scraping it off slices of beef with a spoon so that none of the gristle is included) may be offered in very small quantities a couple of times daily for the first few days. Then by the third day you can mix puppy chow with warm water as directed on the package, offering it four times daily. By now the mother should be kept away from the puppies and out of the box for several hours at a time so that when they have reached five weeks of age she is left in with them only overnight. By the time the puppies are six weeks old, they should be entirely weaned and receiving only occasional visits from their mother.

Most veterinarians recommend a temporary DHL (distemper, hepatitis, leptospirosis) shot when the puppies are six weeks of age. This remains effective for about two weeks. Then at eight weeks of age, the puppies should receive the series of permanent shots for DHL protection. It is also a good idea to discuss with your vet the advisability of having your puppies inoculated against the dreaded parvovirus at the same time. Each time the pups go to the vet for shots, you should bring stool samples so that they can be examined for worms. Worms go through various stages of development and may be present in a stool sample even though the sample does not test positive in every checkup. So do not neglect to keep careful watch on this.

The puppies should be fed four times daily until they are three months old. Then you can cut back to three feedings daily. By the time the puppies are six months of age, two meals daily are sufficient. Some people feed their dogs twice daily throughout their lifetime; others go to one meal daily when the puppy becomes one year of age.

The ideal age for puppies to go to their new homes is between eight and twelve weeks, although some puppies successfully adjust to a new home when they are six weeks old. Be sure that they go to their new owners accompanied by a description of the diet you've been feeding them and a schedule of the shots they have already received and those they still need. These should be included with the registration application and a copy of the pedigree.

One of the breed's truly great bitches. The widely admired Ch. Shinya's Better N' Popcorn, was owned during her show campaigning by Nancy Pritchard and is now owned by her handler Pamela DeHetre. A daughter of American and Canadian Ch. Schauffelein's Vintage Year ex Shinya's Pidgeon English. Bred by Sue Neville.

Chapter 15

Responsibilities of Breeders and Owners

The first responsibility of any person breeding dogs is to do so with care, forethought, and deliberation. It is inexcusable to breed more litters than you need to carry on your show program or to perpetuate your bloodlines. A responsible breeder should not cause a litter to be born without definite plans for the safe and happy disposition of the puppies.

A responsible dog breeder makes absolutely certain, so far as is humanly possible, that the home to which one of his puppies will go is a good home, one that offers proper care and an enthusiastic owner. We have tremendous admiration for those people who insist on visiting (although doing so is not always feasible) the prospective owners of their puppies, to see if they have suitable facilities for keeping a dog, that they understand the responsibility involved, and that all members of the household are in accord regarding the desirability of owning one. All breeders should carefully check out the credentials of prospective purchasers to be sure that the puppy is being placed in responsible hands.

No breeder ever wants a puppy or grown dog he has raised to wind up in an animal shelter, in an experimental laboratory, or as a victim of a speeding car. While complete control of such a situation may be impossible, it is at least our responsibility to make every effort to turn over dogs to responsible people. When selling a puppy, it is a good idea to do so with the understanding that should it become necessary to place the dog in other hands, the purchaser will first contact you, the breeder. You may want to help in some way, possibly by buying or

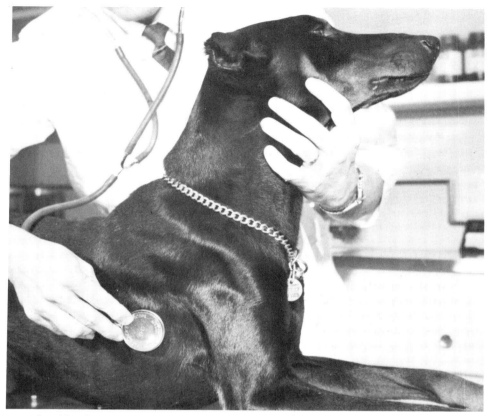

An older dog requires thorough and regular check-ups. The condition of his teeth should be examined more frequently, too.

taking back the dog or placing it elsewhere. It is not fair just to sell our puppies and then never again give a thought to their welfare. Family problems arise, people may be forced to move where dogs are prohibited, or people just plain grow bored with a dog and its care. Thus the dog becomes a victim. You, as the dog's breeder, should concern yourself with the welfare of each of your dogs and see to it that the dog remains in good hands.

The final obligation every dog owner shares, be there just one dog or an entire kennel involved, is that of making detailed, explicit plans for the future of our dearly loved animals in the event of the owner's death. Far too many of us are apt to procrastinate and leave this very important matter unattended to, feeling that everything will work out or that "someone will see to them." The latter is not too likely, at least not to the benefit of the dogs, unless you have done some advance planning which will assure their future well-being.

Life is filled with the unexpected, and even the youngest, healthiest, most robust of us may be the victim of a fatal accident or sudden illness. The fate of our dogs, so entirely in our hands, should never be left to chance. If you have not already done so, please get together with your lawyer and set up a clause in your will specifying what you want done with each of your dogs, to whom they will be entrusted (after first making absolutely certain that the person selected is willing and able to assume the responsibility), and telling the locations of all registration papers, pedigrees, and kennel records. Just think of the possibilities which might happen otherwise! If there is another family member who shares your love of the dogs, that is good and you have less to worry about. But if your heirs are not dog-oriented, they will hardly know how to proceed or how to cope with the dogs themselves, and they may wind up disposing of or caring for your dogs in a manner that would break your heart were you around to know about it.

In our family, we have specific instructions in each of our wills for each of our dogs. A friend, also a dog person who regards her own dogs with the same concern and esteem as we do ours, has agreed to take over their care until they can be placed accordingly and will make certain that all will work out as we have planned. We have this person's name and phone number prominently displayed in our van and car and in our wallets. Our lawyer is aware of this fact. It is all spelled out in our wills. The friend has a signed check of ours to be used in case of an emergency or accident when we are travelling with the dogs; this check will be used to cover her expense to come and take over the care of our dogs should anything happen to make it impossible for us to do so. This, we feel, is the least any dog owner should do in preparation for the time our dogs suddenly find themselves without us. There have been so many sad cases of dogs unprovided for by their loving owners, left to heirs who couldn't care less and who disposed of them in any way at all to get rid of them, or left to heirs who kept and neglected them under the misguided idea that they were providing them "a fine home with lots of freedom." All of us *must* prevent any of these misfortunes befalling our own dogs who have meant so much to us!

The health and physical fitness of a Doberman are just as important as those of your children for a long and fruitful life.

Chapter 16

Diseases and First Aid

The dog is heir to many illnesses; and, as with man, it seems that when one dread form has been overcome by some specific medical cure, another quite as lethal takes its place. It is held by some that this cycle will always continue, since it is Nature's basic way of controlling population.

There are, of course, several ways to circumvent Dame Nature's lethal plans. The initial step in this direction is to put the health of your dog in the hands of one who has the knowledge and equipment to cope competently with canine health problems. We mean, of course, a modern veterinarian. Behind this man are years of study and experience and a knowledge of all the vast research, past and present, which has developed the remarkable cures and artificial immunities that have so drastically lowered the canine mortality rate.

Put your trust in the qualified veterinarian and "beware of Greeks bearing gifts." Beware, too, of helpful friends who say, "I know what the trouble is and how to cure it. The same thing happened to my dog." Home doctoring by unskilled individuals acting upon the advice of unqualified "experts" has killed more dogs than distemper.

Your puppy is constantly exposed to innumerable diseases transmitted by flying and jumping insects, parasites, bacteria, fungus, and virus. His body develops defenses and immunities against many of these diseases, but there are many more which we must cure (or immunize him against) if we want him to live his full span.

You are not qualified to treat your dog for many illnesses with the skill or knowledge necessary for success. This book can only give you a summary of modern findings on the most prevalent diseases and illnesses so that you can, in some instances, eliminate them or the causative agent by yourself. Even more important, this chapter will help you recognize disease symptoms in time to seek the aid of your veterinarian.

Many illnesses have an incubation period, during the early stages of which the animal himself may not show the symptoms of the disease but can readily infect other dogs with which he comes in contact. It is readily seen, then, that places where many dogs are gathered together are particularly dangerous to your dog's health.

Parasitic diseases, which we will first consider, must not be taken too lightly, though they are the easiest of the diseases to cure. Great suffering and even death can come to your pup through these parasites if you neglect to realize the importance of both the cure and the control of reinfestation.

External Parasites

Fleas

The lowly flea is one of the most dangerous insects from which you must protect your dog. It carries and spreads tapeworm, heartworm, and bubonic plague, causes loss of coat and weight, spreads skin disease, and brings untold misery to its poor host. These pests are particularly difficult to combat because their eggs—of which they lay thousands—can lie dormant for months, hatching when conditions of moisture and warmth are present. Thus you may think you have rid your dog (and your house) of these devils, only to find that they mysteriously reappear as weather conditions change.

When your dog has fleas, use any good commercial flea powder. Dust him freely with the powder. It is not necessary to cover the dog completely, since the flea is active and will quickly reach a spot saturated with the powder and die. Whatever specific you use should be used on your dog's sleeping quarters as well as on the animal itself. Repeat the treatment in ten days to eliminate fleas which have been newly hatched from dormant eggs.

Ticks

There are many kinds of ticks, all of which go through similar stages in their life process. At some stage in their lives they all find it necessary to feed on blood. Luckily, these little vampires are fairly easily controlled. The female of the species is much larger than the male, which will generally be found hiding under the female. Care must be taken in the removal of these pests to guard against the mouth parts remaining embedded in the host's skin when the body of the tick is removed. Ether or nail-polish remover, touched to the individual tick, will cause it to relax its grip and fall off the host. The heated head of a match from which the flame has been just extinguished, employed in the same fashion, will cause individual ticks to release their hold and fall from the dog. After veterinary tick treatment, no attempt should be made to remove the pests manually, since the treatment will cause them to drop by themselves as they succumb.

Mites

There are three basic species of mites that generally infect dogs: the demodectic mange mite (red mange), the sarcoptic mange mite (white mange), and the ear mite. Demodectic mange is generally recognized by balding areas on the face, cheeks, and the front parts of the foreleg, which present a moth-eaten appearance. Reddening of the skin and great irritation occurs as a result of the frantic rubbing and scratching of affected parts by the animal. Rawness and thickening of the skin follows. Not too long ago this was a dread disease in dogs, from which few recovered. It is still a persistent and not easily cured condition unless promptly diagnosed and diligently attended to.

Sarcoptic mange mites can infest you as well as your dog. The resulting disease is known as scabies. This disease very much resembles dry dermatitis, or what is commonly called "dry eczema." The coat falls out and the denuded area becomes inflamed and itches constantly.

Ear mites, of course, infest the dog's ear and can be detected by an accumulation of crumbly dark brown or black wax within the ear. Shaking of the head and frequent scratching at the site of the infestation accompanied by squeals and grunting also is symptomatic of the presence of these pests. Canker of the ear is a condition, rather than a specific disease, which covers a wide range of ear infections and which displays symptoms similar to ear mite infection.

All three of these diseases and ear canker should be treated by your veterinarian. By taking skin scrapings or wax particles from the ear for microscopic examination, he can make an exact diagnosis and recommend specific treatment. The irritations caused by these ailments, unless immediately controlled, can result in loss of appetite and weight and can so lower your dog's natural resistance that he is open to the attack of other diseases which his bodily defenses could normally battle successfully.

Internal Parasites

It seems strange, in the light of new discovery of specific controls for parasitism, that the incidence of parasitic infestation should still be almost as great as it was years ago. This can only be due to lack of realization by the dog owner of the importance of initial prevention and control against reinfestation. Strict hygiene must be adhered to if pups are not to be immediately reinfested. This is particularly true where worms are concerned.

In attempting to rid our dogs of worms, we must not be swayed by amateur opinion. The so-called "symptoms" of worms may be due to many other reasons. We may see the actual culprits in the animal's stool, but even then it is not wise to worm indiscriminately. The safest method to pursue is to take a small sample of your puppy's stool to your veterinarian. By a fecal analysis he can advise just what specific types of worms infest your dog and what drugs should be used to eliminate them.

Do not worm your puppy because you "think" he should be wormed or because you are advised to do so by some self-confessed "authority." Drugs employed to expel worms can prove highly dangerous to your pup if used indiscriminately and carelessly, and in many instances the same symptoms that are indicative of the presence of internal parasites can also be the signs of some other affliction.

A word here in regard to that belief that garlic will "cure" worms. Garlic is an excellent flavoring agent, favored by gourmets the world over, *but* it will not rid your dog of worms. Its only curative power lies in the fact that, should you use it on a house dog who has worms, the first time he pants in your face you will definitely be cured of ever attempting this pseudo-remedy again.

Roundworms

These are the most common worms found in dogs and can have grave effects upon puppies, which they almost invariably infest. Potbellies, general unthriftiness, diarrhea, coughing, lack of appetite, and anemia are the symptoms. They can also cause verminous pneumonia when in the larval stage. Fecal examinations of puppy stools should be made by your veterinarian frequently if control of these parasites is to be constant. Although, theoretically, it is possible for small puppies to be naturally worm free, actually most pups are born infested or contract the parasitic eggs at the mother's teat.

The roundworm lives in the intestine and feeds on the pup's partially digested food, growing and laying eggs which are passed out in the pup's stool to be picked up by him in various ways and so cause reinfestation. The life history of all the intestinal worms is a vicious circle, with the dog the beginning and the end host. This worm is yellowish white in color and is shaped like a common garden worm, pointed at both ends. It is usually curled when found in the stool. There are several different species of this type of worm. Some varieties are more dangerous than others. They discharge toxin within the pup, and the presence of larvae in important internal sections of the pup's body can cause death.

With most of the worm drugs, give no food to the dog for twenty-four hours, or in the case of puppies, twenty hours, previous to the time he is given the medicine. It is absolutely essential that this starvation limit be adhered to, since the existence of the slightest amount of food in the stomach or intestine can cause death. A second treatment should follow in two weeks.

Hookworms

These tiny leeches who live on the blood of your dog, which they get from the intestinal walls, cause severe anemia, groaning, fits, diarrhea, loss of appetite and weight, rapid breathing, and swelling of the legs. The same treatment used to eradicate roundworms will also expel hookworms.

Good food is essential for quick recovery, with added amounts of liver and raw meat incorporated in the diet. Blood transfusions are often necessary if the infestation has been heavy. If one infestation follows another, a certain degree of immunity to the effects of the parasite seems to be built up by the dog. A second treatment should be given two weeks following the initial treatment.

Whipworms

These small, thin whiplike worms are found in the intestines and the caecum. Those found in the intestines are reached and killed by the same drugs used in the eradication of roundworms and hookworms. Most worm medicines will kill these helminths if they reach them, but those which live in the caecum are very difficult to reach. They exude toxins which cause debilitation, anemia, and allied ills and are probably a contributing factor in lowering the resistance to the onslaught of other infections. The usual symptoms of worm infestation are present.

233

Tapeworms

Tapeworms are not easily diagnosed by fecal test, but they are easily identified when visible in the dog's stool. The worm is composed of two distinct parts, the head and the segmented body. It is pieces of the segmented body that we see in the stools of the dog. They are usually pink or white, and flat. The common tapeworm, which is most prevalent in our dogs, is about 18" long, and the larvae are carried by the flea. The head of the worm is smaller than a pinhead and attaches itself to the intestinal wall. Contrary to general belief, the puppy infested with tapeworms does not possess an enormous appetite—rather it fluctuates from good to poor. The animal shows the general signs of worm infestation. Often he squats and drags his hindquarters on the ground. This is due to tapeworm larvae moving and wriggling in the lower bowels. One must be careful in diagnosing this symptom, as it may also mean that the dog is suffering from distended anal glands.

No worm medicine can be considered 100 percent effective in all cases. If one drug does not expel the worms satisfactorily, then another must be tried.

Heartworm

This villain inhabits the heart and is the most difficult to treat. The worm is about a foot long and literally stuffs the heart of the affected animal. Unfortunately, it is common, and it has long been the curse of sporting-dog breeds. The worm is transmitted principally through the bite of an infected mosquito, which can fly from an infected canine visitor directly to your dog and do its dire deed.

The symptoms are fatigue, gasping, coughing, nervousness, and sometimes dropsy and swelling of the extremities. Treatment for heartworms definitely must be left in the hands of your veterinarian. A wide variety of drugs are used in treatment. Danger exists during cure when dying adult worms move to the lungs, causing suffocation, or when dead adult worms, in a heavily infested dog, block the small blood vessels in the heart muscles. The invading microfilariae are not discernible in the blood until nine months-following introduction of the disease by the bite of the carrier mosquito.

In an article on this subject in *Field and Stream* magazine, Joe Stetson describes a controlled experiment in which caracide was employed in periodic treatments as a preventive of heartworm. The experiment was carried out over a period of eighteen months, during which time the untreated dogs became positive for heartworm and eventually died. A post-mortem proved the presence of the worm. The dogs that underwent scheduled prophylaxis were found, by blood test, to be free of circulating microfilariae and thrived.

Coccidiosis

This disease is caused by a single-celled protozoa. It affects dogs of all ages, but it is not dangerous to mature animals. When puppies become infected by a severe case of coccidiosis, it very often proves fatal, since it produces such general weakness and emaciation that the puppy has no defense against other invading harmful organisms. Loose and bloody stools are indicative of the presence of this disease, as are loss of appetite, weakness, emaciation, discharge from the eyes, and a fever of approximately 103 degrees. The disease is contracted directly or through flies that have come from infected quarters. Infection seems to occur over and over again, limiting the puppy's chance of recovery with each succeeding infection. The duration of the disease is about three weeks, but new infestations can stretch this period of illness on until your puppy has little chance to recover. Strict sanitation and supportive treatment of good nutrition—utilizing milk, fat, kaopectate, and bone ash with added dextrose and calcium—seem to be all that can be done in the way of treatment. Force feed the puppy if necessary. The more food that you can get into him to give him strength until the disease has run its course, the better will be his chances of recovery.

Your veterinarian can prescribe medication for this disease.

Skin Diseases

Diseases of the skin in dogs are many, varied, and easily confused by the puppy owner. All skin afflictions should be immediately diagnosed and treated by your veterinarian. Whatever drug is prescribed must be employed diligently, and in quantity, and generally long after surface indications of the disease have ceased to exist. A surface cure may be attained, but the infection remains buried deep in the hair follicles or skin glands, to erupt again if treatment is suspended too soon. Contrary to popular belief, diet, if well balanced and complete, is seldom the cause of skin disease.

Eczema

The word "eczema" is a much-abused word, as is the word "dermatitis." Both are used with extravagance in the identification of various forms of skin disorders. We will concern ourselves with the two most prevalent forms of so-called eczema, namely wet eczema and dry eczema. In the wet form, the skin exudes moisture and then scabs over, due to constant scratching and biting by the dog at the site of infection. The dry form manifests itself in dry patches which irritate and itch, causing great discomfort to the dog. In both instances the hair falls out and the spread of the disease is rapid. The cause of these diseases is not yet known, though many are thought to be originated by various fungi and aggravated by allergic conditions. The quickest means of bringing these diseases under control is through the application of a good skin remedy often combined with a fungicide, which your veterinarian will prescribe. An overall dip, employing specific liquid medication, is beneficial in many cases and has a continuing curative effect over a period of days.

Ringworm

This infection is caused by a fungus and is highly contagious to humans. In the dog it generally appears on the face as a round or oval spot from which the hair has fallen. Contact your veterinarian for a cure.

Acne

Your puppy will frequently display small eruptions on the soft skin of his belly. These little pimples rupture and form a scab. The rash is caused by inflammation of the skin glands and is not a serious condition. Treatment consists of washing the affected area with alcohol or witch hazel, followed by the application of a healing lotion or powder.

Hookworm Larvae Infection

The skin of your pup can become infected from the eggs and larvae of the hookworm acquired from a muddy hookworm-infested run. The larvae become stuck to his coat with mud and burrow into the skin, leaving ugly raw red patches. One or two baths in warm water to which an antiseptic has been added usually cures the condition quickly.

Deficiency Diseases

These diseases, or conditions, are caused by dietary deficiencies or some condition which robs the diet of necessary ingredients. Anemia, a deficiency condition, is a shortage of hemoglobin. Hookworms, lice, and any disease that depletes the system of red blood cells are contributory causes. A shortage or lack of specific minerals or vitamins in the diet can also cause anemia. Not so long ago, rickets was the most common of the deficiency diseases, caused by a lack of one or more of the dietary elements (vitamin D, calcium, and phosphorus). There are other types of deficiency diseases originating in dietary inadequacy and characterized by unthriftiness in one or more phases. The cure exists in supplying the missing food factors to the diet. Sometimes, even though all the necessary dietary elements are present in the food, some are destroyed by improper feeding procedure. For example, a substance in raw eggs, avertin, destroys biotin, one of the B-complex group of vitamins. Cooking will destroy the avertin in the egg white and prevent a biotin deficiency in the diet.

Bacterial Diseases

In this group we find leptospirosis, tetanus, pneumonia, strep infections, and many other dangerous diseases. The mortality rate is generally high in all of the bacterial diseases, and treatment should be left to your veterinarian.

Leptospirosis

Leptospirosis is spread most frequently by the urine of infected dogs, which can infect for six months or more after the animal has recovered from the disease. Rats are the carriers of the bacterial agent which produces this disease. A puppy will find a bone upon which an infected rat has urinated, chew the bone, and become infected with the disease in turn. Leptospirosis is primarily dangerous in the damage it does to the kidneys. Complete isolation of affected individuals to keep the disease from spreading and rat control are the chief means of prevention. Also, vaccines may be employed by your veterinarian as a preventive measure. Initial diagnosis is difficult, and the disease has generally made drastic inroads before a cure is effected. It has been estimated that fully 50 percent of all dogs throughout the world have been stricken with leptospirosis at one time or another and that in many instances the disease was not recognized for what it was. The disease produced by *Leptospira* in the blood of humans is known as Weil's disease.

Tetanus

Lockjaw bacteria produce an exceedingly deadly poison. The germs grow in the depths of a sealed-over wound where oxygen cannot penetrate. To prevent this disease, every deep wound acquired by your dog should be thoroughly cleansed and disinfected, and an antitoxin should be given to the animal. Treatment follows the same general pattern as prevention. If the jaw locks, intravenous feeding must be given.

Strep throat

This is a very contagious disease caused by a specific group of bacteria labeled "streptococcus." Characteristic of this disease is the high temperature that accompanies infection (104 to 106 degrees). Other symptoms are loose stool at the beginning of the disease and a slight optic discharge. The throat becomes intensely inflamed, swallowing is difficult, and the glands under the ears are swollen. Immunity is developed by the host after the initial attack.

Tonsillitis

Inflammation of the tonsils can be either of bacterial or virus origin. It is not a serious disease in itself, but it is often a symptom of other diseases. Tonsillitis is not to be confused with strep throat, which is produced by an entirely different organism. The symptoms of tonsillitis are enlarged and reddened tonsils, poor appetite, vomiting, and optic discharge. The disease usually runs its course in from five to seven days. Penicillin, Aureomycin, Terramycin, and Chloromycetin have been used with success in treatment.

Pneumonia

Pneumonia is a bacterial disease of the lungs of which the symptoms are poor appetite, optic discharge, coughing, and shallow and rapid respiration. Affected animals become immune to the particular type of pneumonia from which they have recovered. Early treatment with antibiotics is important, as are proper diet and good nursing care. Immediately consult your veterinarian if your dog exhibits symptoms of this disease.

Viral Diseases

The dread viral diseases are caused by the smallest organisms known to man. They live in the cells and often attack the nerve tissue. The tissue thus weakened is easily invaded by many types of bacteria. Complications then set in, and it is these accompanying ills which usually prove fatal. The secondary infections can be treated with several of the "wonder" drugs, and excellent care and nursing is necessary if the stricken animal is to survive. Your veterinarian is the only person qualified to aid your pup when a viral disease strikes. The diseases in this category include distemper, hepatitis, rabies, leptospirosis, parvovirus, kennel cough, and primary encephalitis—the latter actually inflammation of the brain, a condition characterizing several illnesses, particularly those of viral origin.

Distemper

Until recently a great many separate diseases had been lumped under the general heading of distemper. In the last few years modern science has isolated a number of separate diseases of the distemper complex, such as infectious hepatitis, hard-pad disease, influenza, and primary encephalitis, which had been diagnosed as distemper. Thus, with more accurate diagnosis, great strides have been made in conquering not only distemper, but also these other, allied diseases. Distemper (Carre) is now rare, due to successful methods of immunization, but any signs of illness in an animal not immunized may be the beginning of the disease. The symptoms are so similar to those of various other diseases that only a trained observer can diagnose correctly. Treatment consists of the use of drugs to counteract complications arising from the invasion of secondary diseases and in keeping the stricken animal warm, well fed, comfortable, and free from dehydration until the disease has run its course. In many instances, even if the pup gets well, he will be left with some dreadful souvenir of the disease which will mar him for life. Aftereffects are common in most of the diseases of the distemper complex.

The tremendous value of immunization against this viral disease cannot be exaggerated. Except for the natural resistance your animal carries against disease, it is the one means of protection you have against this killer. There are reasonably sure indications that the vaccine protects against hard-pad disease and primary encephalitis as well as distemper. Injections can be given at any age, even as early as six or eight weeks, with a repeat dosage at twelve to sixteen weeks of age. Your dog should then receive annual revaccination.

Hepatitis

This disease attacks dogs of all ages but is particularly deadly to puppies. We see young puppies in the nest, healthy, bright and sturdy; suddenly they begin to vomit, and the next day they are dead of infectious hepatitis—it strikes that quickly. The disease is almost impossible to diagnose correctly, and there is no known treatment that will cure it. Astute authorities claim that if an afflicted dog survives three days after the onslaught of the disease he will, in all probability, completely recover. Research has given us a vaccine that affords safe and effective protection against hepatitis, and the vaccination schedule should be the same as for distemper.

Rabies

This is the most terrible of diseases, since it knows no bounds. It is transmissible to all kinds of animals and birds, including the superior animal, man. To contract this dread disease, the dog must be bitten by a rabid animal or the rabies virus must enter the body through a broken skin surface. The disease incubation period is governed by the distance of the virus point of entry to the brain. The closer the point of entry is to the brain, the quicker the disease manifests itself. We can be thankful that rabies is not nearly as prevalent as is supposed by the uninformed. Restlessness, excitability, perverted appetite, character reversal, wildness, drowsiness, loss of acuteness of senses (and of feeling, in some instances), foaming at the mouth, and many other lesser symptoms come with the onslaught of this disease. Diagnosis by trained persons of a portion of the brain is conceded to be the only way of determining whether an animal died of rabies or of one of the distemper complex diseases. Very little has been done in introducing drugs or specifics that can give satisfaction in combating this disease; perhaps evaluation of the efficacy of such products is almost impossible with a disease so rare and difficult to diagnose.

In 1948 an avianized, modified live virus vaccine was found, and is being used throughout this country today. Quarantine, such as that pursued in England, even of six months' duration, is still not the answer to the rabies question, though it is undeniably effective. It is, however, not proof positive. Recently a dog on arriving in England was held in quarantine for the usual six months. The day before he was to be released to his owners, the attendant noticed that he was acting strangely. He died the next day. Under examination his brain showed typical inclusion bodies, establishing the fact that he had died of rabies. This is a truly dangerous disease that can bring frightful death to animal or man. With an effective way of immunization known and recommended by authoritative sources, it should be the duty of every dog owner to protect his dog, himself, his family, and neighbors from even the slight risk that exists of contracting rabies by taking immediate advantage in this form of protection.

Freedom from skin disease, good diet, and grooming contribute to the beautiful condition of this Doberman's coat.

Leptospirosis

This disease affects the kidneys of our dogs, and it can also affect other domesticated animals as well as man. The organism which causes this disease is carried in the urine of mice and rats and is very resistant to treatment. Symptoms include fever, vomiting, diarrhea, dehydration, and great thirst.

With the development of a vaccine which effectively protects dogs from leptospirosis, this dread disease has been almost completely eradicated. The first inoculation should be given at nine weeks of age, with a repeat dosage at twelve to sixteen weeks of age. Your dog should then receive annual revaccination.

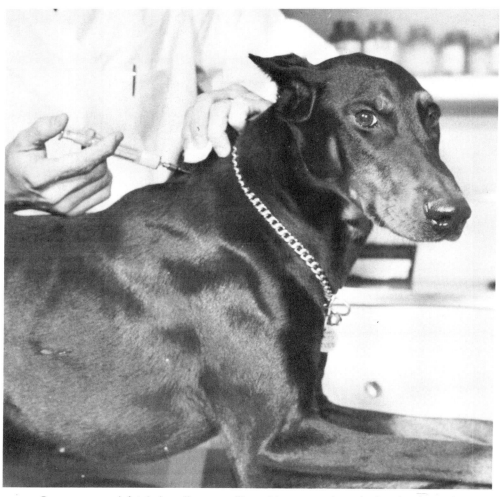
Dangerous and fatal dog diseases, like rabies, parvovirus, leptospirosis, and others are all preventable by the pertinent shots against these ailments.

Parvovirus

This relatively new virus is a contagious disease that has spread in almost epidemic proportions throughout certain sections of the United States. Also, it has appeared in Australia, Canada, and Europe. Canine parvovirus attacks the intestinal tract, white blood cells, and heart muscle. The specific source of infection seems to be fecal matter

242

of infected dogs. Overcoming parvovirus is difficult, for it is capable of existing in the environment for many months under varying conditions and temperatures, and direct contact between dogs is not necessary; it can be transmitted from place to place on the hair and feet of infected dogs, as well as on the clothes and shoes of people.

Vomiting, fever, and severe diarrhea, which will appear within five to seven days after the animal has been exposed to the virus, are the initial signs of this disease. At the onset of illness, feces will be light gray or yellow-gray in color, and the urine might be blood-streaked. Because of the vomiting and severe diarrhea, the dog that has contracted the disease will dehydrate quickly. Depression and loss of appetite can accompany the other symptoms. Death caused by this disease usually occurs within 48 to 72 hours following the appearance of the symptoms. Puppies are hardest hit, and the virus is fatal to 75 percent of puppies that contact it. Death in puppies can be within two days of the onset of the illness.

A series of shots administered by a veterinarian is the best preventive measure for canine parvovirus. It is also important to disinfect the area where the dog is housed by using one part sodium hypochlorite solution (household bleach) to thirty parts of water and to keep the dog from coming into contact with the fecal matter of other dogs.

Kennel Cough

The virus which causes this disease is airborne and the disease itself is highly contagious. It can quickly spread through an entire kennel full of dogs. The virus causes inflammation of the larynx and trachea, and infected dogs begin to cough.

Protection against kennel cough or parainfluenza, in the form of a vaccine given on the same schedule as distemper inoculations, is very important. Because unborn puppies might become infected, though, pregnant bitches should not be given vaccinations against the disease.

Fits

Fits in dogs are symptoms of diseases rather than illness itself. They can be caused by the onslaught of any number of diseases, including worms, distemper, epilepsy, primary encephalitis, and poisoning, among others. Running fits can also be traced to dietary deficiencies. The underlying reason for the fits, or convulsions, must be diagnosed by your veterinarian and the cause treated.

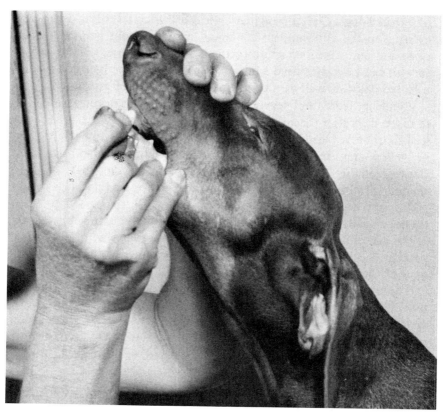

Since the administration of pills is inevitable, learn the technique recommended in this book.

Diarrhea

Diarrhea, which is officially defined as watery movements occurring eight or more times a day, is often a symptom of one of many other diseases. But, if on taking your dog's temperature, you find there is no fever, it is quite possible the condition has been caused by either a change of diet, of climate or water, or even by a simple intestinal disturbance. A tightening agent such as Kaopectate should be given. Water should be withheld and corn syrup, dissolved in boiled milk, substituted to prevent dehydration in the patient. Feed hard-boiled eggs, boiled milk, meat, cheese, boiled white rice, crackers, kibbles, or dog biscuits. If the condition is not corrected within two or three days, if there is an excess of blood passed in the stool, or if signs of other illness become manifest, don't delay a trip to your veterinarian.

Constipation

If the dog's stool is so hard that it is difficult for him to pass it and he strains and grunts during the process, then he is obviously constipated. The cause of constipation is diet. Bones and dog biscuits, given abundantly, can cause this condition, as can any of the items of diet mentioned above as treatment for diarrhea. Chronic constipation can result in hemorrhoids which, if persistent, must be removed by surgery. The cure for constipation and its accompanying ills is the introduction of laxative food elements into the diet. Stewed tomatoes, buttermilk, skim milk, whey, bran, alfalfa meal, and various fruits can be fed and a bland physic given. Enemas can bring quick relief. Once the condition is rectified, the dog should be given a good balanced diet, avoiding all types of foods that will produce constipation.

Eye Ailments

The eyes are not only the mirror of the soul, but they are also the mirror of many kinds of disease. Discharge from the eyes is one of the many symptoms warning of most internal viral, parasitic, and bacterial diseases. Of the ailments affecting the eye itself, the most usual are glaucoma, which seems to be a hereditary disease; pink eye, a strep infection; cataracts; opacity of the lens in older dogs; corneal opacity, such as follows some cases of hepatitis; and teratoma. Mange, fungus, inturned lids, and growths on the lid are other eye ailments. The wise procedure is to consult your veterinarian for specific treatment.

When the eyes show a discharge from reasons other than those that can be labeled "ailment," such as irritation from dust, wind, or sand, they should be washed with warm water on cotton or a soft cloth. After gently washing the eyes, an ophthalmic ointment combining a mild anesthetic and antiseptic can be utilized. Of course, the liquid discharged by the dog's tear ducts is itself a good antiseptic.

Anal Glands

If your male dog consistently drags his rear parts on the ground or bites this area, the cause is probably impacted anal glands. These glands, which are located on each side of the anus, should be periodically cleared by squeezing. The job is not a nice one and can be much more effectively done by your veterinarian. Unless these glands are kept reasonably clean, infection can become housed in this site, resulting in the formation of an abscess which will need surgical care. Dogs that get an abundance of exercise seldom need the anal glands attended to.

The many other ailments which your dog is heir to, such as cancer, tumors, rupture, heart disease, fractures, and the results of accidents, must all be diagnosed and tended to by your veterinarian. When you go to your veterinarian with a sick dog, always remember to bring along a sample of his stool for analysis. Many times samples of his urine are needed, too. Your veterinarian is the only one qualified to treat your dog for disease, but protection against disease is to a great extent in the hands of the dog owner. If those hands are capable, a great deal of pain and misery for both dog and owner can be eliminated. Death can be cheated, investment saved, and veterinary bills kept to a minimum. A periodic health check by your veterinarian is a wise investment.

Administering Medication

Some people seem to have ten thumbs on each hand when they attempt to give medicine to their dog. They become agitated and approach the task with so little sureness that their mood is communicated to the patient, increasing the difficulties. Invite calmness and quietness in the patient by displaying these qualities yourself. Speak to the animal in low, easy tones, petting him slowly, quieting him down in preparation. The administration of medicine should be made without fuss and as though it is some quiet and private new game between you and your dog.

At the corner of your dog's mouth there is a lip pocket perfect for the administering of liquid medicine if used correctly. Have the animal sit; then raise his muzzle so that his head is slanted upward looking toward the sky. Slide two fingers in the corner of his mouth where the upper and lower lip edges join, pull gently outward, and you have a pocket between the cheek flesh and the gums. Into this pocket pour the liquid medicine slowly. Keep his head up, and the liquid will run from the pocket into his throat and he will swallow it. Continue this procedure until the complete dose has been given. This will be easier to accomplish if the medicine has been spooned into a small bottle. The bottle neck, inserted into the lip pocket, is tipped, and the contents will slowly run down his throat.

To give pills or capsules, the head of the patient must again be raised with muzzle pointing upward. With one hand, grasp the cheeks of the pup just behind the lip edges where the teeth come together on the inside of the mouth. With the thumb on one side and the fingers on the other, press inward as though squeezing. The lips are pushed against the teeth, and the pressure of your fingers forces the mouth open. The dog will not completely close his mouth, since doing so would cause him to bite his lips. With your other hand, insert the pill in the patient's mouth as far back on the base of the tongue as you can, pushing it back with your second finger. Withdraw your hand quickly, allow the dog to close his mouth, and hold it closed with your hand, but not too tightly. Massage the dog's throat and watch for the tip of his tongue to show between his front teeth, signifying the fact that the capsule or pill has been swallowed.

In taking your dog's temperature, an ordinary rectal thermometer is adequate. It must be first shaken down, then dipped in petroleum jelly, and inserted into the rectum for approximately three-quarters of its length. Allow it to remain there for no less than a full minute, restraining the dog from sitting during that time. When withdrawn, it should be wiped with a piece of cotton, read, then washed in alcohol—never hot water. The arrow on most thermometers at 98.6 degrees indicates normal human temperature and should be disregarded. Normal temperature for your grown dog is 101 degrees; normal dog temperature varies between 101½ and 102 degrees. Excitement can raise the temperature, so it is best to take a reading only when the dog is calm.

In applying an ophthalmic ointment to the eye, simply pull the lower lid out, squeeze a small amount of ointment into the pocket thus produced, and release the lid. The dog will blink, and the ointment will spread over the eye.

Should you find it necessary to give your dog an enema, employ an ordinary human-size bag and rubber hose. Simply grease the catheter with petroleum jelly and insert the hose well into the rectum. The bag should be held high for a constant flow of water. A quart of warm soapy water or plain water with a tablespoonful of salt makes an efficient enema for a big dog. Puppies need proportionately less.

First Aid

Emergencies quite frequently occur which make it necessary for you to care for the dog yourself until veterinary aid is available. Quite often emergency help by the owner can save the pup's life or lessen the chance of permanent injury. A badly injured animal, blinded to all else but abysmal pain, often reverts to the primitive, wanting only to be left alone with his misery. Injured, panic-stricken, not recognizing you, he might attempt to bite when you wish to help him. Under the stress of fright and pain, this reaction is normal in animals. A muzzle can easily be slipped over his foreface, or a piece of bandage or strip of cloth can be fashioned into a muzzle by looping it around the dog's muzzle, crossing it under the jaws, and bringing the two ends around in back of the dog's head and tying them. Snap a leash onto his collar as quickly as possible to prevent him from running away and hiding. If it is necessary to lift him, grasp him by the neck, getting as large a handful of skin as you can, as high up on the neck as possible. Hold tight and he won't be able to turn his head far enough around to bite. Lift him off the ground by the hold you have on his neck, encircle his body with your other arm, and support him or carry him.

Every dog owner should have handy a first-aid kit specifically for the use of his dog. It should contain a thermometer, surgical scissors, rolls of 3″ and 6″ bandage, a roll of 1″ adhesive tape, a package of surgical cotton, a jar of petroleum jelly, enema equipment, bulb syringe, ten c.c. hypodermic syringe, flea powder, skin remedy, tweezers, ophthalmic ointment, paregoric, Kaopectate, hydrogen peroxide, merthiolate, alcohol, ear remedy, aspirin, milk of magnesia, castor oil, mineral oil, and dressing salve.

Here are two charts for your reference, one covering general first-aid measures and the other a chart of poisons and antidotes. Remember that in most instances these are emergency measures, not specific treatments, and are designed to help you in aiding your dog until you can reach your veterinarian.

FIRST-AID CHART

Emergency	Treatment	Remarks
Accidents	Automobile, treat for shock. If gums are white, indicates probable internal injury. Wrap bandage tightly around body until it forms a sheath. Keep animal very quiet until veterinarian comes.	Call veterinarian immediately.
Bee stings	Give paregoric or aspirin to ease pain. If in state of shock, treat for same.	Call veterinarian for advice.

Bites (animal)	Area of tooth wounds should be shaved and antiseptic solution flowed into punctures, with eyedropper. Iodine, merthiolate, and so on can be used. If badly bitten or ripped, take dog to your veterinarian for treatment.	If superficial wounds become infected after first aid, consult veterinarian.
Burns	Apply ice or very cold water and compresses to burned area, followed by cold packs.	Unless burn is very minor, consult veterinarian immediately.
Broken bones	If break involves a limb, fashion splint to keep immobile. If ribs, pelvis, shoulder, or back involved, keep dog from moving until professional help comes.	Call veterinarian immediately.
Choking	If bone, wood, or any foreign object can be seen at back of mouth or throat remove with fingers. If object can't be removed or is too deeply imbedded or too far back in throat, rush to veterinarian immediately.	
Cuts	Minor cuts: allow dog to lick and cleanse. If not within his reach, clean cut with peroxide, then apply merthiolate. Severe cuts: apply pressure bandage to stop bleeding—a wad of bandage over wound and bandage wrapped tightly over it. Take to veterinarian.	If cut becomes infected or needs suturing, consult veterinarian.
Dislocations	Keep dog quiet and take to veterinarian at once.	
Drowning	Artificial respiration. Lay dog on his side, push with hand on his ribs, release quickly. Repeat every two seconds. Treat for shock.	
Electric shock	Artificial respiration. Treat for shock.	Call veterinarian immediately.
Heat stroke	Quickly immerse the dog in cold water until relief is given. Lay dog flat and pour cold water over him, turn electric fan on him, and continue pouring cold water as it evaporates.	Cold towel pressed against abdomen aids in reducing temperature quickly if quantity of water not available.
Porcupine quills	Tie dog up, hold him between knees, and pull all quills out with pliers. Don't forget tongue and inside of mouth.	See veterinarian to remove quills too deeply embedded.
Shock	Cover dog with blanket. Administer stimulant (coffee with sugar). Allow him to rest, and soothe with voice and hand.	Alcoholic beverages are NOT stimulants.
Snake bite	Cut deep X over fang marks. Drop potassium-permanganate into cut. Apply tourniquet **above bite** if on foot or leg.	Apply first aid only if a veterinarian or a doctor can't be reached.

249

POISON AND ANTIDOTE CHART

Poison	Household Antidote
Acids	Bicarbonate of soda
Alkalies	Vinegar or lemon juice
(cleansing agents)	
Arsenic	Epsom salts
DDT	Peroxide and enema
Food Poisoning	Hydrogen peroxide, followed by enema
(garbage, etc.)	
Hydrocyanic acid	Dextrose or corn syrup
(wild cherry; laurel leaves)	
Lead	Epsom salts
(paint pigments)	
Mercury	Eggs and milk
Phosphorus	Hydrogen peroxide
(rat poison)	
Strychnine	Sedatives. Phenobarbital, Nembutal.
Thallium	Table salt in water
(bug poisons)	
Theobromine	Phenobarbital
(cooking chocolate)	

The important thing to remember when your dog is poisoned is that prompt action is imperative. Administer an emetic immediately. Mix hydrogen peroxide and water in equal parts. Force this mixture down your dog. In a few minutes he will regurgitate his stomach contents. Once this has been accomplished, call your veterinarian. If you know the source of the poison and the container which it came from is handy, you will find the antidote on the label. Your veterinarian will prescribe specific drugs and advise on their use.

The symptoms of poisoning include trembling, panting, intestinal pain, vomiting, slimy secretion from mouth, convulsions, and coma. All these symptoms are also prevalent in other illnesses; but if they appear and investigation leads you to believe that they are the result of poisoning, act with dispatch as described above.

Index

Camera Phone Obsession

Peter G. Aitken

PARAGLYPH™
P R E S S

Camera Phone Obsession

Limits of Liability and Disclaimer of Warranty

The author and publisher of this book have used their best efforts in preparing the book and the programs contained in it. These efforts include the development, research, and testing of the theories and programs to determine their effectiveness. The author and publisher make no warranty of any kind, expressed or implied, with regard to these programs or the documentation contained in this book.

The author and publisher shall not be liable in the event of incidental or consequential damages in connection with, or arising out of, the furnishing, performance, or use of the programs, associated instructions, and/or claims of productivity gains.

Trademarks

Trademarked names appear throughout this book. Rather than list the names and entities that own the trademarks or insert a trademark symbol with each mention of the trademarked name, the publisher states that it is using the names for editorial purposes only and to the benefit of the trademark owner, with no intention of infringing upon that trademark.

Paraglyph Press, Inc.
4015 N. 78th Street, #115
Scottsdale, Arizona 85251
Phone: 602-749-8787
www.paraglyphpress.com

Paraglyph Press ISBN: 1-932111-96-4

Printed in the United States of America
10   9   8   7   6   5   4   3   2   1

President
Keith Weiskamp

Editor-at-Large
Jeff Duntemann

Developmental Editor
Ben Sawyer

Vice President, Sales, Marketing, and Distribution
Steve Sayre

Vice President, International Sales and Marketing
Cynthia Caldwell

Production Manager
Kim Eoff

Cover Designer
Kris Sotelo